THE DAIRY COOKBOOK

THE DAIRY COOKBOOK

Olga Nickles

CELESTIAL ARTS
Millbrae, California

First Printing, October 1976
Made in the United States of America

Library of Congress Cataloging in Publication Data

Nickles, Olga, 1932–
  The dairy cookbook.

  1. Cookery (Dairy products) I. Title.
TX759.N5   641.6'7   76-11345
ISBN 0-89087-172-8

1 2 3 4 5 6 7 8 – 81 80 79 78 77 76

In memory of my grandmother, Eugenia Chronis

THANKS . . .
to my husband, Achilles, for all his help . . . to my
children, Nina, Michael, and Georgia, for their
smiling faces . . . to my parents, George and
Stamatia Loukides, for teaching me the basics.

CONTENTS

*I flew over Greenland
and it looked like one big yogurt.*

Bob Hope

YOGURT

When my husband and I moved from New Jersey to Iowa City, Iowa, in 1960, I assumed that I would be able to buy yogurt in the supermarkets there, just as I had done back East. I was disappointed! There was no yogurt for sale. In fact, there were very few Midwesterners who had even heard of it.

Being of Greek descent, I had been eating yogurt all my life, so it came as a surprise when I realized that here was a dairy food that wasn't part of the American kitchen.

A year later we took a trip to Wisconsin to visit friends. To our delight we were given a supply of *maya* or yogurt starter. It was like a treasure to us. Carefully we took it home to Iowa City where I used it to make a batch of wonderful-tasting yogurt.

To many Americans, yogurt is a novel food, although it has been a staple in the Old World for thousands of years. Yogurt has the effect of preserving milk, often for long periods of time. This is still a matter of great nutritional importance in such places as India and the Middle East, which lack modern food-distribution and cold storage facilities. For generations, in Southeastern Europe, the Far East, and Central Asia, yogurt has formed and still forms a part of the people's everyday diet.

There's a true story of how I learned the Indian name for yogurt. A friend from India was visiting and after an evening of talking and drinking, my husband woke up the next morning with a terrible hangover. Our Indian friend volunteered that he could cure it. He kept asking for *dahi* and it took a while until I realized that what he needed was yogurt. It seems that yogurt, made into a drink by adding a little water and herbs, is believed capable of working "the cure." Perhaps, but after trying the yogurt cure, my husband says he'd rather endure the hangover.

That evening while we were talking with our Indian friend about yogurt, he explained that in a large country such as India, their *dahi* varies in taste and quality not only from region to region but within different districts of the same large city. In India there is no such thing as a standard yogurt.

However, if a Bulgarian heard this he would shake his head in disbelief. Just as, for a Frenchman, Roquefort cheese can only be made in a special area of France, so for a Bulgarian, yogurt can only be made in his country. Only Bulgaria's mountains, he will tell you, have the right climate and atmosphere to produce the Lactobacillus Bulgaricus, the fermenting organism that curdles milk in just the right way to turn it into yogurt. In Bulgaria, yogurt is made from a

3

combination of goat's milk and water buffalo's milk, a mixture which is twice as rich in butterfat as the yogurt we know.

Maybe it was the yogurt each Bulgarian consumed; or Bulgaria's climate; or the character of the bacillus that bears its name, but whatever the reason, it is a fact that in the early 1900's Bulgaria, with a population of less than three million, could count about 145 centenarians for every one in the United States.

Dr. Elie Metchnikoff, a Russian bacteriologist from Kharkov, who eventually became director of the Pasteur Institute in Paris, was the first to isolate and identify the yogurt bacillus. This was the crucial step that made it possible to control the manufacture of yogurt on a large scale.

This doctor, a cowinner in 1908 of the Nobel Prize for Physiology and Medicine, was particularly interested in the subject of longevity. He believed that a human life span of 150 years was not an unreasonable expectation. Inevitably he was fascinated by the large number of centenarians in Bulgaria, and sought the reason for this in the quantities of yogurt they consumed.

He followed their example, making yogurt an important part of his diet, but unfortunately he died at 71. Nevertheless, the yogurt he loved has gone on to become more popular than even he had hoped.

In the 1930's yogurt was so little known in the Western World that a number of reliable dictionaries published at the time make no reference to it. Yet today, more yogurt is eaten in France than in any other country. According to one source, Frenchmen have polished off 1.7 *billion* pots of yogurt in a single year. And its popularity has spread to Canada, where consumption increased 450 percent within a recent three-year period. Here in the U.S. approximately 420 million pounds of yogurt was consumed in 1975 according to the United Dairy Industry Association.

In this country, three developments turned yogurt into a booming business. American tourists sampled it abroad and liked it; Gaylord Hauser promoted it as a health food; and a small agressive company advertised heavily to educate the public about yogurt. At first, surveys showed, this company had almost no competition, or market either. But by the mid 1940's America was finally introduced to yogurt.

Sometimes the taste of a particular food can bring back a flood of memories. The taste of yogurt reminds me of my childhood when I was growing up in Plainfield, New Jersey. It seemed there was always a culture of yogurt being prepared in my grandmother's kitchen. It was rare indeed not to see a pile of woolen sweaters wrapped around the earthen pot in which the yogurt was fermenting. This was how she had learned to make yogurt in her native Greece. As I sat at the wooden table enjoying the wonderful smells of her cooking, Nené, as we called her, would pour honey over our servings of yogurt, cut slices of her freshly made bread, pour me a glass of unhomogenized milk and fill her demitasse with thick Turkish coffee. Then sometimes while we ate, she would tell me about the virtues of yogurt, and in my blissful innocence I never thought that any family, anywhere, could live without it.

As has happened to me, and surely to other yogurt-lovers, people who do not eat yogurt often gasp in disbelief when they learn that others do eat it. Here is your chance to surprise these ill-informed abstainers by serving them a whole meal using yogurt in every course. Listen to their praises, and only then tell them your secret.

A final note to the yogurt cook; use this book as a guide, but don't be limited by it. Experiment and have fun.

NOW THAT YOU ASK....

Q. Is yogurt something new?
A. It's at least four thousand years old. There is evidence that the Egyptians were familiar with yogurt and the Chinese too. There is also a biblical reference to the serving of cultured milk.

Q. Then why haven't I heard much about it?
A. Although yogurt has been very popular in Europe and Asia for a long time, it wasn't introduced commercially into the United States until the 1940's.

Q. How is yogurt spelled?
A. Various ways, including yaourt, yoghoort, yoghourt, yoghurt, yogourt. But the "yogurt" spelling is easy to pronounce and has become the accepted form in the United States.

Q. Where does that strange word come from?
A. Turkey.

Q. Do all countries use the Turkish word?
A. By no means. To order yogurt in any of the following countries, use its local name.

Dahi - India	Mezzoradu - Sweden
Filmjolk - Sweden	Plimae - Finland
Kaelder milk - Norway	Skyr - Iceland
Koumiss - Central Asia	Yaourti or oxygala - Greece
Laban or mast - Egypt	Yoghei - Holland
Madzoon - Armenia	Yoghourt - France
Mast - Iran	Yogurt - Bulgaria
	Varenetz or prostokvasha - Russia

Q. What is yogurt anyway?
A. It is a fermented, slightly acid, semi-fluid milk food, made of milk to which bacteria cultures have been added. It contains natural enzymes and is sometimes called a "living food."

Q. By "milk" do you mean cow's milk?

A. Not exclusively. Yogurt can be made from the milk of the water buffalo, sheep, camel, reindeer, mare or goat. But in the United States commercial yogurt is made only from cow's milk.

Q. Is yogurt harder to digest than milk?

A. It is easier to digest than milk because of the digestive action of yogurt bacilli on milk protein. It is considered an ideal food for both babies and elderly persons who cannot assimilate ordinary milk.

Q. What vitamins does yogurt contain?

A. It is richer in the living B-complex vitamins, because yogurt bacilli "grade up" and diversify milk protein, actually producing more B-vitamins than found in whole milk.

Q. What other beneficial substances does it contain?

A. It is rich in calcium, which is made more readily available by the action of lactic acid. It is also an excellent source of protein and minerals.

Q. Does plain yogurt contain much sugar?

A. No, because a large part of the sugar that is present in milk ferments into acid, alcohol, or gas.

Q. How can yogurt be prevented from curdling when used in cooking?

A. In a saucepan, combine 1 teaspoon of cornstarch with 1 tablespoon of yogurt. Blend well. Add 1 cup of yogurt and bring the mixture to a simmer over low heat. Cook for about 10 minutes or until thickened. Stir occasionally. After the mixture has cooled, blend until smooth.

Q. What is yogurt's calorie content?

A. The calories per half-pint range from about 130 for plain yogurt to about 260 for the so-called Swiss-style varieties, in which fruit preserves are blended into the yogurt. Because it satisfies hunger, but is low in calories, yogurt is becoming a popular and valuable dieting aid.

Q. Sometimes yogurt looks watery on top. Does that mean it's spoiled?

A. No. You may find after you have taken some yogurt from its container and refrigerated what is left, some of the whey (a watery substance) will separate from the curd. Don't be alarmed. Just tip the container a little and spoon out the excess liquid.

Q. Can I freeze yogurt?

A. You can freeze the fruit-flavored kind. If the fruit is at the bottom it should be stirred before freezing. Plain yogurt should not be frozen.

Q. Can yogurt be made at home?

A. Easily. The straight, no-nonsense method is discussed in detail in the section beginning on page 8.

Q. But don't you need special equipment?

A. No. But yogurt-making equipment does exist for those who want it. See the section just mentioned.

Q. Aside from food, can yogurt be put to any other use?

A. One cosmetologist recommends it as a cosmetic mask. The idea goes back to ancient Persia where women used yogurt as a facial to coddle their complexions, and where it was esteemed as an ointment for sunburns also.

Q. I've heard that you can get drunk on yogurt. Is that possible?

A. Hardly. Some "cultured milks" pack a milk kick, but the strongest is *busa*, a Turkestani drink that is seven percent alcohol. In Chile a similar tipple is called *skuta*, or "whey champagne."

Q. Is there any relationship between yogurt and sex?

A. Nothing has been proved, but why not try yogurt and see?

MAKE YOUR OWN YOGURT

Some feel that making yogurt calls for a special knack but actually the process is easy and undemanding. For instance, the milk can be heating while you prepare other foods and it can be cooling while you do other chores.

Yogurt *is* simple to make but the technique requires some practice before it is mastered. The first three steps are easy to summarize: heat the milk until it comes to a boil, cool to 110°-115°, then add the yogurt starter. After that, the important thing to remember is that yogurt needs a consistently warm place in which to "set" because it is sensitive to temperature changes. The best temperature for this "setting" period is approximately 90° to 120°.

Although not quite scientific I have found that my grandmother's method works best for me. I pour the prepared milk into an earthen bowl (or into glasses or jars), cover with paper towels to absorb excess moisture, and set the bowl or containers on the kitchen counter, away from any draft. Then I cover everything with a clean kitchen towel and finally wrap the bowl or containers with a woolen sweater or a small woolen blanket. The mixture is allowed to "set" undisturbed for six hours.

Another method for "incubating" the prepared milk is to preheat the oven to 120° for five minutes, then turn it off. Put the containers of yogurt in a pan, cover tops with paper towels, and place them in the oven until they set, about six hours.

Still another way is to preheat an insulated picnic box by letting jars of warm water stand in it for ten minutes. Remove the jars, put in containers, cover the box with its top, and keep it closed for six hours.

These are but a few of the methods used in "incubating" the yogurt as it sets. You may find a variation that suits you better which is fine as long as the temperature remains between 90° to 120° throughout the process.

Try to use the freshest milk you can buy to make yogurt. You can use whole milk or skim milk; it doesn't matter, but the tastes will be different with the type of milk used. If a richer yogurt is desired, add one cup of heavy cream to the milk. Skim milk will make yogurt with less butterfat, if that is a consideration. Following are recipes for yogurt using whole milk, skim milk, and evaporated milk.

Occasionally you may not be lucky. Instead of ending up with yogurt, you may still have milk. This can happen when the culture you used was an old or stale one, the milk may have been turning sour, or the temperature during incubation may have been too high or too low. In such cases, I feel that it is best to throw out the whole batch and start over.

After all this, if you still lack confidence, consider buying an electric yogurt-maker which is designed to hold constant temperatures. You set the dial and let the thermostat control the heat. Personally, I'm divided about the use of yogurt-making devices. They work well and they do take the guesswork out of the warming period. Yet somehow I derive a pleasant feeling from using warm sweaters and blankets to cover the incubating yogurt. It gives me a sense of time and tradition.

Another modern approach to yogurt making is a commercial dry culture that can be used as a starter. It has the advantage of needing no refrigeration and is useful if you want to make up some yogurt away from home.

No matter how you go about your yogurt-making, don't be surprised to find that each batch has a subtly different taste from all the others. These variations are characteristic of homemade yogurt, so you will be enjoying a continually new taste experience.

The basic recipes that follow can be varied by adding different flavors to the yogurt after it has been refrigerated. For instance, stir in a cup of diced fresh fruit or berries sweetened to taste with sugar or honey. If you add preserves, no sweetening is necessary. To make honey yogurt, stir three tablespoons of honey into the milk before you heat it.

Every batch you make will taste so good that you will want to eat it all. But don't. Remember to save and refrigerate two tablespoons for use as a starter the next time.

BASIC YOGURT RECIPE

1 quart milk
2 tablespoons plain yogurt, homemade or commercial (this is called the starter)

Bring starter to room temperature. Pour milk into a heavy pot. Heat milk until it reaches 180° on candy thermometer. Stir often with a wooden spoon so that no top skin forms. (If you do not have a thermometer, let the milk come to a boil

and cook for 5 minutes, stirring constantly.) Cool to 110-115°, stirring occasionally. (When you can hold your little finger in the milk for a slow count of ten, the milk has cooled sufficiently.) Thin starter with 4 tablespoons of the cooled milk, add to the pot and stir to blend. Pour mixture into an earthen pot or individual serving dishes. Cover. Keep mixture warm and undisturbed for 5 to 6 hours. This is essential. When mixture has reached a thick consistency, refrigerate.
Yield: Four 8-oz. servings.

SKIM MILK YOGURT RECIPE

1 quart skim milk
1 cup powdered skim milk

3 tablespoons plain yogurt, home-
    made or commercial

Bring starter to room temperature. Pour skim milk into a heavy pot. Heat milk to 115°, but do not boil. Remove from heat. Add powdered skim milk and yogurt. Stir to blend. Continue as in basic yogurt recipe.
Yield: Five 8-oz. servings.

EVAPORATED MILK YOGURT RECIPE

6 cups lukewarm water
1½ cups powdered skim milk

3 tablespoons plain yogurt, home-
    made or commercial
1 13-oz. can evaporated milk

In a large pot, combine and mix well 2 cups of the water, the powdered skim milk, and the yogurt. Add remaining water and evaporated milk and mix again. Heat to 115°. Do not boil. Continue as in basic yogurt recipe.
Yield: Eight 8-oz. servings.

THE MANY WAYS OF YOGURT

Sweeten plain yogurt with sugar and a few drops of vanilla extract.
Sprinkle yogurt with cinnamon.
Serve with stewed cherries, crushed strawberries, fresh sliced peaches or apricots.
Mix plain yogurt with applesauce, raisins, chopped walnuts, or shredded coconut.
Mix vanilla yogurt with any fruit preserve.

Mix equal amounts of cottage cheese and yogurt.

Top breakfast cereals with fruit-flavored yogurt.

Mix yogurt with chopped fresh parsley as a topping for baked potatoes.

Use it as a topping for pickled herring.

Combine a can of drained tuna fish or drained salmon with yogurt.

Flavor plain yogurt by adding a little minced garlic, dill, or celery.

Serve on top of rice or cooked vegetables.

Top honeydew or melon balls with scoops of yogurt.

Mix with sliced radishes, cucumbers, onions, peppers, or celery.

Mix 1 cup of coffee yogurt with 2 tablespoons of brandy for a sauce over slices of sponge cake.

Pour honey, pancake syrup, or chocolate syrup over yogurt.

Use it as a topping for baked apples.

Yogurt can be given a thicker consistency, like that of cottage cheese, by the following method:

Make a container out of three or four layers of cheesecloth. Place it in a large bowl, pour 2 to 4 cups of yogurt into it, pull up the corners and tie the ends together. Hang the resultant bag over the bowl, or over the kitchen sink, to drain for a few hours or overnight, depending on consistency desired. The longer the yogurt drains, the thicker it will become. The result is called "yogurt curds" and may be used like cottage cheese. Salt lightly to taste, chill and serve mixed with chives or other herbs, or with canned peaches or pineapple.

For a yogurt-like pudding, add 6 tabelspoons sugar to 2 cups yogurt curds, blend, and whip thoroughly. Serve cold.

DIPS AND APPETIZERS

Try substituting yogurt for the sour cream in the dip for your next party. There are 490 calories in one cup of sour cream and only 130 calories in one cup of plain yogurt.

For another change, serve your yogurt dips with crisp raw vegetables, such as carrot curls, tiny raw mushrooms, cauliflower flowerets, and even raw turnips or zucchini cut in slices or sticks.

AVOCADO DIP

1 medium avocado, peeled	**Worcestershire sauce, a dash**
Salt to taste	**½ cup yogurt**

In a mixing bowl, mash the pulp of the avocado. Add salt and Worcestershire

sauce. Fold in yogurt; mix until light and well blended. Serve with corn chips or sesame crackers.
Yield: about 1½ cups.

BLUE RIBBON DIP

3 tablespoons blue cheese,
  crumbled

1 cup yogurt
½ teaspoon salt

Mix all ingredients. Chill. Serve with sesame crackers or wheat wafers.
Yield: about 1¼ cups.

CAVIAR DIP

1 4-oz. jar red caviar
1 teaspoon chopped chives

1 tablespoon lemon juice
1 cup yogurt

Combine caviar, chives, and lemon juice. Fold mixture into yogurt and chill. Serve with small wheat biscuits.
Yield: about 1½ cups.

CHEDDAR-CHEESE NUT BALL

3 cups finely grated Cheddar cheese
⅓ cup crumbled blue cheese
½ cup yogurt
½ teaspoon Worcestershire sauce

¼ cup pitted, minced, green olives
½ cup chopped walnuts
¼ cup chopped fresh parsley

Beat Cheddar and blue cheese together until smooth. Add yogurt and Worcestershire sauce; mix until creamy. Add olives. Cover and refrigerate 3 to 4 hours. Combine chopped walnuts and parsley. Shape cheese mixture into a ball; then roll in nuts and parsley. Return to refrigerator until ready to serve. Slice and serve on crackers or thin pumpernickel slices.
Yield: 1 cheese nut ball.

CHILI YOGURT DIP

½ cup cottage cheese
¼ cup chili sauce
1 tablespoon chili seasoning mix

1 teaspoon horseradish
½ teaspoon salt
½ cup yogurt

Beat cottage cheese with chili sauce until smooth. Add chili seasoning mix, horse-radish, and salt. Fold in yogurt. Chill. Serve with iced cucumber or green pepper strips.
Yield: about 1¼ cups.

COTTAGE-CHEESE DIP*

½ cup cottage cheese
1 tablespoon grated carrot
1 teaspoon finely chopped green
  pepper

2 teaspoons grated onion
Salt to taste
⅛ teaspoon garlic salt
1 cup yogurt

In a mixing bowl, beat cottage cheese for at least 2 minutes. Add vegetables, salt, and garlic salt and beat until smooth. Fold in yogurt. Cover and refrigerate. Serve as a dip for raw vegetables.
Yield: about 1½ cups.

*A low-calorie dip: approximately 50 calories per ¼ cup serving.

GOLDEN CHEESE APPETIZERS

1 cup Mazola oil
2 cups all-purpose flour
1 egg yolk

1 cup yogurt
⅛ teaspoon salt
Confectioners' sugar

Filling:
  1 cup grated Romano or Parmesan
    cheese
  2 egg yolks

1 tablespoon flour
½ cup cottage cheese

Glaze:
  1 egg white
  ½ teaspoon milk

Preheat oven to 350°. Beat oil for 5 minutes. Work in flour and egg yolk. Add yogurt and, if necessary, more flour to produce a soft dough that can be rolled easily. Roll out the dough until very thin. Using a 3-inch cookie cutter or a tea-cup, cut dough into circles. Mix ingredients for filling. Place 1 teaspoon filling on each circle of dough. Bring the sides up and seal by pressing. Make glaze by beating egg white and milk together. Use to brush each appetizer. Bake until golden brown, about 25 minutes. Remove from oven and sprinkle with confec-tioners' sugar.
Yield: about 4 dozen appetizers.

CHUTNEY DIP

1 cup yogurt
1 teaspoon curry powder
2 tablespoons chutney

Salt to taste
Pepper to taste

Mix all ingredients thoroughly. Cover and chill. Serve with crackers.
Yield: 1 cup.

MARINATED MUSHROOMS*

1 pound fresh mushrooms
4 cups water
2 tablespoons salt
1 tablespoon vinegar
¼ cup chopped onion
2 tablespoons chopped parsley
2 tablespoons lemon juice

1 tablespoon vinegar
2 teaspoons sugar
¼ teaspoon thyme
¼ teaspoon salt
¼ teaspoon pepper
¾ cup yogurt

Carefully clean mushrooms; slice. In a saucepan bring water, 2 tablespoons salt, and 1 tablespoon vinegar to a boil. Add mushrooms. Cover. Simmer for 10 minutes. Drain. Cool. In a large bowl, combine onion, parsley, lemon juice, 1 tablespoon vinegar, sugar, thyme, ¼ teaspoon salt, and pepper. Add yogurt and mushrooms, mix and cover bowl. Marinate in refrigerator about 12 hours, preferably overnight.
Yield: about 2 cups.

*A low-calorie appetizer: approximately 65 calories per ½ cup serving.

MEDITERRANEAN APPETIZER

1 medium eggplant
¾ cup olive oil
1 clove garlic, minced

1 teaspoon salt
1 cup yogurt

Peel eggplant and slice thinly. Sprinkle slices with salt and stack them up. Let stand about 1 hour, then rinse and dry. Heat oil in skillet and sauté slices, a few at a time until golden brown on both sides. Drain on absorbent paper. Place slices in a serving dish. Combine garlic, salt, and yogurt, and pour over eggplant slices. Chill. Serve with feta cheese, black olives, and Syrian bread.
Yield: 6 servings.

PISTACHIO DIP

2 3-oz. packages softened cream
  cheese
¼ cup crumbled blue cheese
½ cup yogurt

1 teaspoon lemon juice
¼ teaspoon salt
3 tablespoons pistachio nuts

Beat cream cheese and blue cheese together until fairly smooth. Fold in yogurt, lemon juice, and salt. Add pistachio nuts. Cover and chill. Serve with crackers. *Yield: about 1½ cups.*

YOGURT WINE DIP

2 teaspoons white wine
2 teaspoons finely chopped onions
1 teaspoon mustard

½ cup cooked ham, finely chopped
1 cup yogurt

Mix all ingredients thoroughly. Cover and chill. Serve with crackers or sesame wafers.
Yield: 1½ cups.

SALADS 'N' DRESSINGS

An appealing salad enhanced by yogurt and served with crisp salad greens should whet any appetite. You can add almost any herbs or seasoning to your salads made with yogurt such as dill, caraway seed, curry powder, or chili powder.

Using some imagination, you can combine yogurt with various fruits and vege-tables, often with gelatin, to make a complete course. The acidity of yogurt, by the way, will keep a cut avocado or sliced peaches from oxidizing. Besides being low in calories, yogurt adds a tangy flavor to salad dressings.

Here are a few hints in serving any dressing at its best. Make it a few hours beforehand so that its flavors have time to blend. If it turns out too thick, thin it with a little milk. Remember to serve dressings at room temperature.

AMBROSIA DELIGHT

2 tablespoons honey
1 tablespoon lemon juice
2 oranges, peeled, sectioned, and
  membrane removed
1 apple, diced

1 banana, sliced
1 peach, diced
1 cup shredded coconut
1 cup fruit-flavored yogurt

Combine honey and lemon juice. Add fruits and coconut; mix. Refrigerate. When ready to serve, add yogurt, toss gently, and serve immediately.
Yield: 4 servings.

APPLE-CABBAGE SLAW*

1 tablespoon vinegar
1 teaspoon caraway seed
1 teaspoon prepared mustard
½ teaspoon salt
⅛ teaspoon garlic salt
1 cup yogurt

1½ cups coarsely chopped unpeeled apple
Lemon juice
4 cups shredded cabbage
⅛ cup chopped celery

In a mixing bowl, combine vinegar, caraway seed, mustard, salt, and garlic salt. Fold in yogurt. Cover and chill. Coat chopped apple with lemon juice, then add to cabbage and celery. Before serving, toss solid ingredients with seasoned yogurt.
Yield: 4 servings.

*A low-calorie salad: approximately 100 calories per serving.

AUTUMN SALAD

1 teaspoon sugar
½ teaspoon salt
½ teaspoon grated lemon rind
¼ teaspoon cinnamon
1 cup apricot-flavored yogurt

3 cups unpeeled chopped apples
1 cup chopped celery
½ cup chopped walnuts
½ cup white raisins

Combine the first four ingredients. Fold in yogurt. In a salad bowl, mix apples, celery, walnuts, and raisins. Toss gently with yogurt dressing, cover, and chill.
Yield: 6 to 8 servings.

AVOCADO-ORANGE SALAD

1 3-oz. package lime flavored gelatin
1 cup boiling water
1 ripe avocado
1 tablespoon lemon juice
½ teaspoon salt

1 cup yogurt
¾ cup small curd cottage cheese
1 orange, peeled and diced
¼ cup chopped walnuts or pecans
1 11-oz. can mandarin orange slices (optional)

Dissolve gelatin in hot water. Refrigerate until partly set. Peel and mash avocado with lemon juice and salt. Combine avocado, yogurt, cottage cheese, orange, and nuts; fold into gelatin. Pour mixture into a 1-quart mold. Chill until firm. Unmold. Garnish with mandarin orange slices.
Yield: 4 to 6 servings.

CABBAGE SALAD*

1 medium cabbage, shredded
1 cup yogurt
1 cup crushed pineapple, drained

2 medium carrots, shredded
2 teaspoons cider vinegar
Salt to taste

Combine all ingredients and toss lightly. Chill.
Yield: 8 servings.

*A low-calorie salad: approximately 70 calories per serving.

CALIFORNIA SALAD

¾ teaspoon dill weed
½ teaspoon salt
¾ cup yogurt
1 cup cooked, chopped shrimp
½ cup unpeeled, chopped cucumber

½ cup grated carrot
¼ cup chopped celery
1 small onion, sliced
3 ripe avocados
Lemon juice

Combine dill weed, salt, and yogurt. Cover and refrigerate. Combine shrimp, cucumber, carrots, celery, and onions. Cut avocados in half and rub cut surface with lemon juice. When ready to serve, fold yogurt into shrimp mixture and spoon into avocado halves.
Yield: 6 servings.

CUCUMBER SALAD*

1 cucumber, peeled and thinly sliced
½ teaspoon salt
1 tablespoon chopped fresh parsley
½ garlic clove, minced
1 medium onion, thinly sliced

1 teaspoon sugar
1 tablespoon vinegar
1 tablespoon salad oil
½ cup yogurt
Dash of pepper

Sprinkle sliced cucumber with salt and refrigerate at least 2 hours. Combine re-

maining ingredients, cover and chill. When ready to serve, rinse cucumber with cold water, pat dry; then combine with yogurt mixture.
Yield 4 servings.

*A low-calorie salad: approximately 75 calories per serving.

NATURE'S BOUNTY SALAD

1 cup yogurt
2 tablespoons soy sauce
½ head romaine lettuce
3 large mushrooms
2 medium carrots
1 ripe avocado
Lemon juice
1 cup raw peas

1 cauliflower, divided into small
  flowerets
½ cup shelled pumpkin seeds
½ cup shelled sunflower seeds
¼ cup toasted sesame seeds
½ cup raisins
½ cup raw, broken cashews

In a small bowl, combine yogurt and soy sauce. Refrigerate. Wash and dry lettuce leaves. Arrange them on bottom of a large salad bowl. Cut mushrooms and carrots into thin strips. Place strips in a circle in center of the salad bowl. Peel and slice avocado. Sprinkle with lemon juice to prevent discoloration. Arrange avocado and remaining ingredients around mushrooms and carrot strips. Top with yogurt-soy sauce dressing.
Yield: 4 to 6 servings.

POTATO SALAD*

1 tablespoon horseradish
1 teaspoon salt
½ teaspoon mustard
1 cup yogurt
4 cups cooked and diced potatoes

½ cup chopped celery
¼ cup chopped green pepper
¼ cup chopped onion
1 tablespoon chopped pimento

In a mixing bowl, combine horseradish, salt, and mustard. Fold in yogurt. In a salad bowl, mix potatoes, celery, green pepper, onion, and pimento. Pour yogurt dressing over potato mixture and toss lightly.
Yield: 6 servings.

*A low-calorie salad: approximately 100 calories per serving.

SUMMER ISLANDER

2 cantaloupes
2 oranges, peeled and sectioned
1 cup seedless grapes
¾ cup pitted sliced dates
½ cup yogurt

1 teaspoon orange rind
2 teaspoons honey
Dash of salt
Shelled sunflower seeds for garnish

Cut cantaloupes in half, and remove seeds. Combine oranges, grapes, and dates. Spoon mixture into cantaloupe halves. Combine yogurt, orange rind, honey, and salt; then place a spoonful on each serving. Garnish with sunflower seeds. *Yield: 4 servings.*

SUNSHINE SALAD*

2 1-pound cans grapefruit sections
Grapefruit juice
2 envelopes unflavored gelatin
¼ teaspoon salt

⅔ cup shredded carrots
⅔ cups diced celery
1 cup yogurt

Drain grapefruit sections; reserve. Add grapefruit juice to syrup to make 3 cups. Sprinkle gelatin over 1 cup of the liquid in saucepan to soften. Place over low heat, stirring constantly, until gelatin is dissolved. Remove from heat. Add remaining 2 cups grapefruit liquid and salt. Chill to consistency of unbeaten egg whites. Fold in drained grapefruit sections, shredded carrots, celery, and yogurt. Turn into 6-cup mold and chill until firm. *Yield: 6 servings.*

*A low-calorie salad: approximately 85 calories per serving.

FROZEN PEACH SALAD

1 16-oz. can sliced peaches
½ cup peach syrup
1 cup small marshmallows
1 8-oz. package cream cheese

¼ cup sugar
¼ teaspoon salt
1 cup cherry-flavored yogurt

Drain peaches, saving ½ cup syrup. Place syrup and marshmallows in a saucepan and cook over low heat, stirring occasionally, until marshmallows are melted. Cool slightly. In a mixing bowl, beat cream cheese until smooth. Add sugar and salt and beat until light and fluffy. Add cooled marshmallow mixture and beat

until well blended. Combine yogurt and peaches and fold into cream-cheese mixture. Pour into refrigerator trays (or into an 8-inch square pan) and freeze until set. Remove from freezer for at least an hour before serving.
Yield: 6 to 8 servings.

ALL-PURPOSE SALAD DRESSING

1 cup yogurt
½ cup mayonnaise

½ teaspoon salt
4 teaspoons sugar

Mix all ingredients thoroughly. Chill.
Yield: 1½ cups.

BLUE CHEESE DRESSING

¼ cup crumbled blue cheese
1 teaspoon wine vinegar
½ teaspoon sugar

¼ teaspoon salt
1 cup yogurt

In a salad bowl, crush blue cheese with a fork. Add vinegar, sugar, and salt. Fold in yogurt and mix lightly. Serve chilled on a green salad.
Yield: about 1¼ cups.

CANDIED-GINGER DRESSING

1 cup yogurt
4 teaspoons lemon juice

2 tablespoons finely chopped candied
  ginger
Salt to taste

Combine all ingredients and chill. Serve over cottage cheese or fruit salads.
Yield: about 1¼ cups.

CURRY DRESSING

1 cup yogurt
¼ cup finely chopped celery leaves
¼ cup chopped fresh parsley
¼ cup mayonnaise
3 scallions, minced

1 tablespoon prepared horseradish
1 teaspoon salt
2 teaspoons sugar
1 teaspoon curry powder
¼ cup lemon juice.

Beat all ingredients together to a smooth consistency. Chill. Serve on a tossed salad.
Yield: 1½ cups.

DIJON DRESSING*

1 cup yogurt   ¼ cup finely chopped chives
1 tablespoon fresh lemon juice   1 teaspoon dijon mustard
1 garlic clove, finely chopped   Salt and pepper to taste

Combine all ingredients. Spoon over sliced tomatoes or a green salad.
Yield: about 1¼ cups.

*A low-calorie dressing: approximately 8 calories per serving.

FLUFFY FRUIT DRESSING

2 cups yogurt   2 egg yolks
2 egg whites   6 tablespoons sugar

24 hours before serving, pour yogurt into a colander which has been lined with several layers of cheesecloth. Set colander over a bowl to drain. Before serving, beat egg whites until soft peaks form. In another bowl, combine egg yolks and sugar. Beat until thick and yellow. (More sugar may be added if desired.) Place drained yogurt in a bowl. Fold egg yolk-sugar mixture into the yogurt; then fold in beaten egg whites. Serve on salads of canned or fresh fruit.
Yield: about 2½ cups.

GOLDEN ORANGE DRESSING

1 cup vanilla-flavored yogurt   2 teaspoons honey
2 cups cottage cheese   ⅓ cup orange juice

Mix all ingredients thoroughly. Chill. Serve on salads of canned or fresh fruit.
Yield: 3⅓ cups.

SAVORY DRESSING*

1 cup yogurt   1 hard-boiled egg, chopped
1 tablespoon lemon juice   ¼ teaspoon prepared mustard
¼ teaspoon celery seed   ½ teaspoon salt

Mix all ingredients. Chill 30 minutes or more.
Yield: about 1¼ cups.

*A low-calorie dressing: approximately 10 calories per serving.

SESAME-HONEY DRESSING

2 tablespoons honey
2 tablespoons toasted sesame seeds
1 teaspoon grated orange rind
1 teaspoon grated lemon rind
⅛ teaspoon salt
1 cup orange-flavored yogurt

Combine honey, sesame seeds, orange rind, lemon rind, and salt. Fold in yogurt and chill. Serve on fresh-fruit salad.
Yield: 1¼ cups.

TANGY SALAD DRESSING

1 cup yogurt
2 cups mayonnaise
2 tablespoons lemon juice
4 to 6 tablespoons Roquefort cheese

Mix all ingredients well and chill. Serve on a tossed-green salad.
Yield: 3½ cups.

TAYLOR'S YOGURT DRESSING*

1 cup yogurt
2 tablespoons lemon juice
1 teaspoon salt
1 teaspoon Worcestershire sauce
½ teaspoon dry mustard
3 teaspoons grated onion
2 tablespoons chopped parsley
Dash cayenne

Mix all ingredients well. Serve on cold meats, aspics, and fish.
Yield: about 1½ cups.

*A low-calorie dressing: approximately 10 calories per serving.

SOUPS

Cucumbers and yogurt seem to go together naturally. The cool fragrance of cucumbers combines with the tartness of yogurt to make a light, refreshing summer soup that needs no cooking. Yogurt also blends well with chicken stock or with any other meat or fish stock you may have on hand.

BARLEY SOUP

½ cup pearl barley
4 cups chicken broth
2 medium onions, chopped
2 tablespoons butter

1 teaspoon dried mint (optional)
1 tablespoon chopped fresh parsley
Salt and pepper to taste
2 cups yogurt

Cover barley with water and soak overnight. Drain barley and stir into chicken broth. Simmer for about 15 minutes or until barley is tender. Sauté onion in butter until soft. Add to broth. Add mint, parsley, salt, and pepper to taste. Simmer 30 minutes longer. Five minutes before serving, remove from heat. Mix a little hot broth into yogurt, and pour into soup. Serve in heated bowls.
Yield: 6 servings.

CABBAGE SOUP*

8 cups water
1 small cabbage, shredded
1 small onion, chopped
1 16-oz. can tomatoes
1 teaspoon salt

½ teaspoon pepper
1 tablespoon lemon juice
4 teaspoons sugar
1 cup yogurt

Bring water to a boil. Add cabbage and onion. Cover tightly and cook over low heat for 30 minutes. Add tomatoes, salt, pepper, lemon juice, and sugar. Cover and cook over low heat for 1 hour. Serve hot. Top each bowl with a generous portion of yogurt.
Yield: 6 to 8 servings.

*A low-calorie dish: approximately 70 calories per one cup serving.

CUCUMBER SOUP*

3 medium cucumbers
1 garlic clove, peeled
1 cup yogurt
1 tablespoon lemon juice

1 tablespoon fresh mint, chopped
½ teaspoon salt
Pepper to taste
3 teaspoons fresh dill, chopped

Peel cucumber and chop into fine pieces. Cut garlic clove in half and use cut surface to rub soup bowls. Combine cucumber, yogurt, lemon juice, mint, salt, and pepper. Stir well. Place in soup bowls and garnish with dill.
Yield: 4 servings.

*A low-calorie dish: approximately 50 calories per one cup serving.

GREEN GODDESS SOUP

1 ripe avocado
1 10½-oz. can condensed cream of
  chicken soup
2⅓ cups milk
1 cup yogurt

1 cup cooked ham, finely chopped
1 cup light cream
1 tablespoon lemon juice
½ teaspoon salt
¼ teaspoon pepper

Peel and remove seed from avocado. Cut into small pieces. Place avocado and all other ingredients into a mixing bowl and stir to a smooth consistency. Refrigerate 2 to 4 hours. If a thinner soup is desired, add a little more milk.
Yield: 4 to 6 servings.

NOODLE SOUP

1 egg
3 cups yogurt
1 teaspoon salt
2 cups water
1 cup egg noodles, broken

2 tablespoons butter
1 small onion, finely chopped
2 teaspoon dry mint, crushed
  (optional)

In a large saucepan, beat egg, yogurt, and salt 3 minutes. Add water. Bring mixture to a boil over high heat, stirring constantly. Lower heat. Add noodles, stir and cook until tender. In a frying pan, sauté the onions until light brown. Add mint. Blend onions and mint into soup; simmer for 5 minutes.
Yield: 6 servings.

SHRIMP CHOWDER

1 medium cucumber
1 cup yogurt
1½ cups chicken stock
1 cup tomato juice
1 garlic clove, crushed
2 teaspoons lemon juice
2 teaspoons chopped fresh dill

½ cup cooked shrimp
1 tomato, peeled, seeded, and diced
2 tablespoons chopped green pepper
1 cup light cream
Salt and pepper to taste
Chopped fresh dill for garnish

Peel and slice cucumber. Place in a bowl, sprinkle with salt, cover with a towel for 30 minutes. Drain and rinse with cold water. Place yogurt, stock, tomato juice, and garlic into an electric blender and blend until smooth. Pour mixture into a serving bowl. Add lemon juice, dill, cucumber, shrimp, tomato, and green pepper. Stir in cream. Season with salt and pepper to taste. Chill. Garnish with dill.
Yield: 4 to 6 servings.

YOGURT-RICE SOUP

5 cups chicken stock
3 tablespoons rice
2 tablespoons butter
1 cup yogurt

2 tablespoons flour
2 tablespoons fresh chopped parsley
Salt and pepper to taste

Bring chicken stock to a boil. Add rice and cook until tender, about 20 minutes. Melt butter in a saucepan. Add yogurt and flour to butter and cook over low heat, stirring, until thick and smooth. Blend sauce into chicken stock. Add parsley, salt, and pepper to taste.
Yield: 4 servings.

MAIN DISHES

With yogurt you can give main dishes an unusual touch. Chicken and lamb can be marinated in yogurt with delicious results. Rice topped with yogurt suddenly becomes a Mediterranean delight.

Here are recipes for the cook who will try something different.

CRUNCHY CHICKEN

1 cup pineapple-flavored yogurt
1 chicken, cut in serving pieces
1 cup wheat germ
1½ teaspoons chopped fresh parsley

¼ teaspoon thyme
¼ teaspoon basil
Salt and pepper to taste
2 tablespoons butter

Heat oven to 350°. Place yogurt in a bowl. Wash chicken pieces and pat dry. Dip chicken pieces in yogurt and coat both sides thoroughly. Combine wheat germ,

parsley, thyme, basil, salt, and pepper. Melt butter to grease the bottom of large baking dish. Roll yogurt-coated chicken in wheat-germ mixture and place in baking dish. Bake for 1 hour.
Yield: 4 servings.

MARINATED CHICKEN

1 chicken, cut in serving pieces
1 cup yogurt
2 garlic cloves, crushed
½ teaspoon ground ginger
¼ cup fresh lime juice
2 teaspoons ground coriander
1 teaspoon ground cumin
½ teaspoon cayenne pepper
¼ teaspoon aniseed
4 tablespoons butter
Lime wedges for garnish

Wash chicken pieces and pat dry. Combine all ingredients except last two. Marinate in refrigerator for at least 24 hours. Place chicken on greased rack in baking pan and roast in 350° oven for 1½ hours or until tender. Baste occasionally with melted butter. Garnish with lime wedges.
Yield: 4 servings.

POLYNESIAN CHICKEN

1 teaspoon salt
3 tablespoons flour
1 chicken, cut in serving pieces
2 tablespoons butter
1 medium onion, chopped
1 12½-oz. can mandarin orange
  sections
½ cup liquid from oranges
½ cup water
Salt and pepper to taste
1 cup mandarin-orange yogurt

Combine salt and 2 tablespoons of the flour and use to dredge chicken pieces. In a large skillet, melt butter and brown chicken. Remove chicken from pan. Add onion and cook until soft. Drain mandarin orange sections, reserving the liquid. Return chicken to skillet, add reserved juice, water, salt, and pepper. Cover. Simmer for 45 minutes or until chicken is tender. Place chicken on serving dish and keep warm. Blend remaining tablespoon flour with 1 tablespoon of pan liquid and stir into liquid remaining in skillet. Cook, stirring constantly, until mixture comes to a boil. Add yogurt and orange slices and stir well. Heat through. Pour yogurt sauce over chicken.
Yield: 6 servings.

SPECIAL CHICKEN

1 teaspoon chili powder	Juice of one lemon
¼ teaspoon ground ginger	1 tomato, peeled, seeded and chopped
2 garlic cloves	1 chicken, cut in serving pieces
½ cup unsweetened grated coconut	¼ cup peanut oil
¼ cup slivered blanched almonds	2 medium onions, sliced
1 cup yogurt	1 teaspoon salt

In a blender, grind chili powder, ginger, garlic, coconut, and almonds. In a large bowl, combine blended mixture with yogurt, lemon juice, and tomatoes. Add chicken, making sure that each piece is coated. Cover and marinate for at least 2 hours. In an uncovered baking dish, heat oil on top of stove and sauté onions until soft. Add chicken, marinade, and salt and bring to a simmer. Cover and bake at 325° for 1½ hours.
Yield: 6 servings.

BEEF STROGANOFF

1½ pounds top sirloin of beef	2 tablespoons flour
4 tablespoons butter	2 tablespoons water
4 cups sliced fresh mushrooms	1 cup yogurt
1 large onion, thinly sliced	Salt and pepper to taste
¼ cup warm brandy	

Cut the beef into strips about 3-inches long and ½-inch thick. Melt 2 tablespoons of the butter in a skillet and sauté mushrooms until golden. Remove and set aside. Add remaining 2 tablespoons butter to the skillet and sauté steak strips until brown. Push meat to one side, and sauté onions until soft. Return mushrooms to skillet; combine with meat and onions. Pour brandy over all and ignite. In a mixing bowl, combine flour and water until smooth. Blend in yogurt. Combine sauce with steak and mushrooms. Cook over low heat, stirring constantly until mixture thickens and comes to a boil. Cover and simmer for 3 minutes. Season with salt and pepper.
Yield: 6 servings.

DOLMATHES*
(STUFFED GRAPE LEAVES)

1 pound ground lamb or beef	Salt and pepper to taste
1 medium onion, chopped	About 50 canned grape leaves
½ cup uncooked rice	1½ cups chicken broth
¼ cup chopped fresh parsley	1½ cups water
½ teaspoon dried mint	1 cup yogurt

Mix beef, onion, rice, parsley, mint, salt, and pepper. Rinse grape leaves in hot water to remove excess brine. Line bottom of saucepan with a few grape leaves to prevent scorching. Fill each leaf, coarse side up, with one teaspoon of meat mixture. Roll carefully, tucking in edges to seal contents completely. Place stuffed leaves, seam side down, in saucepan, making more than one layer. Add chicken broth and water. Weight leaves with a heavy plate to keep them in place. Cover and simmer 1 hour or longer, until rice is tender, adding more liquid if necessary. Serve hot, topped with yogurt.
Yield: about 6 servings.

*A low-calorie dish: approximately 290 calories per serving.

LITTLE MEAT PIES

3 8-oz. packages refrigerator
   biscuits
1½ pounds ground lean beef or lamb
2 medium onions, finely chopped

½ cup yogurt
½ cup pine nuts (optional)
Salt and pepper to taste

Preheat oven to 350°. Roll out each biscuit. Combine meat, onions, yogurt. Season to taste. Place a tablespoon of mixture on each biscuit patty. Fold over edges, leaving center open. Place meat patties on an oiled baking sheet. Bake 20 minutes or until lightly browned. Serve hot.
Yield: 3 dozen meat pies.

MEXICAN JAMBOREE

1 tablespoon butter
1½ pounds ground beef
¾ cup chopped onion
1 garlic clove, minced
1½ cups grated Cheddar cheese
1 15 oz. can enchilada sauce

1 1-pound can kidney beans, drained
¾ teaspoon salt
½ teaspoon chili powder
2 cups crushed corn chips
1 cup yogurt

In a large frying pan, melt butter and sauté beef, onion, and garlic until beef is browned. Add Cheddar cheese, enchilada sauce, kidney beans, salt, and chili powder. Stir to mix. Turn off heat. In a baking dish, place half the corn chips. Spread meat mixture over chips. Spoon yogurt over meat in little mounds. Top with remaining corn chips and bake 8 minutes at 350°.
Yield: 6 to 8 servings.

LAMB ON WHOLE-WHEAT BREAD

¼ cup olive oil
1 medium onion, finely chopped
1 teaspoon salt
5 crushed peppercorns
4 lamb steaks

4 slices whole-wheat bread
½ cup hot beef broth
3 cups yogurt
Paprika

Combine olive oil, onion, salt, and peppercorns. Put lamb steaks in a shallow dish and cover with olive oil mixture. Leave to marinate 2 to 3 hours. Drain meat and broil to degree desired. In the meantime, toast bread and place on a heat-proof serving dish. Pour hot beef broth over toast and place dish in a warm oven until slices absorb liquid completely. Just before serving, heat yogurt over low fire, stirring frequently. Place a shank on each slice of bread and pour yogurt sauce over all. Sprinkle with paprika.
Yield: 4 servings.

OLD-FASHIONED LAMB STEW

1 tablespoon butter
1 pound lean lamb, cut in cubes
1 teaspoon salt
1 teaspoon pepper
¾ teaspoon dill weed
2 cups water

5 medium potatoes
4 medium carrots
4 stalks celery
1 cup yogurt
2 tablespoons flour

Melt butter in a large skillet and brown lamb on all sides. Add salt, pepper, dill weed, and water. Cover. Cook over low heat 1 hour or until meat is almost tender. Peel and quarter potatoes, scrape and cut carrots in 2-in. pieces, wash and cut celery in 2-in. pieces. Add vegetables to lamb. Simmer for 30 minutes longer or until vegetables are cooked. Remove meat and vegetables and keep warm. Combine yogurt and flour. Add to pan juices and cook over low heat until thickened. Stir often. Arrange lamb and vegetables on a serving platter and pour yogurt gravy over all.
Yield: 4 servings.

SPICED LAMB AND RICE*

3 tablespoons butter
2 pounds lamb, cut in 1-inch cubes
2 cups yogurt
2 teaspoons salt
1 medium onion, chopped
3 teaspoons curry powder
1½ cups uncooked rice

3 whole cloves
¼ teaspoon chili powder
⅛ teaspoon cinnamon
1 10½-oz. can condensed beef consomme
½ cup hot water

In a skillet, melt butter and brown lamb cubes over high heat. Transfer lamb to a large bowl. Mix yogurt and salt. Add to meat. Place onion and curry in same skillet and sauté until onion is soft. Add lamb mixture to skillet. Stir in rice. Add cloves, chili powder, cinnamon, consomme, and hot water. Bring to a boil. Reduce heat, cover and simmer 20 minutes. Uncover. Stir thoroughly. Cover again and simmer 10 more minutes or until rice is tender.
Yield: 6 servings.

*A low-calorie dish: approximately 480 calories per serving.

HAM AND NOODLE CASSEROLE

1 8-oz. package medium noodles
3 cups cooked ham, cubed
1 cup yogurt
1 cup cottage cheese
1 cup grated Cheddar cheese

2 tablespoons pimento strips
(optional)
1 teaspoon caraway seed
¾ teaspoon salt
¼ teaspoon garlic powder

Preheat oven to 350°. Cook noodles according to package directions. Drain and place in a large mixing bowl. Add remaining ingredients and combine thoroughly. Butter a 2-quart casserole and pour in noodle mixture. Bake 35 to 45 minutes.
Yield: 4 to 6 servings.

PORK BAKE WITH ORANGE RICE

4 to 5 pounds loin of pork
1 cup yogurt
1 tablespoon chopped onion
1 tablespoon peanut oil

3 teaspoons curry powder
2 teaspoons salt
½ teaspoon ground ginger
¼ teaspoon ground cardamon

Orange Rice:
1¼ cups water
1¼ cups orange juice

1 cup uncooked rice
1 teaspoon grated orange rind

Place pork loin in a deep bowl, fat side up. Combine yogurt, onion, oil, curry, salt, ginger, and cardamon. Rub mixture over pork loin. Cover and marinate in refrigerator 24 hours. Preheat oven to 325°. Place pork on rack in a shallow roasting pan and bake 2½ hours. Serve with orange rice.
Yield: 6 servings.

Orange Rice:
Bring water and orange juice to a boil. Add rice, salt, and grated orange rind. Cover tightly and cook over low heat until all liquid is absorbed, about 25 minutes.

GOURMET LOBSTER THERMIDOR

½ pound lobster tails
2 tablespoons butter
¼ cup finely chopped celery
1½ tablespoons flour
¼ teaspoon salt
1 cup milk
1 egg, beaten

½ cup yogurt
1 2-oz. can mushrooms, drained
  and sliced
½ teaspoon grated lemon rind
½ teaspoon prepared mustard
2 tablespoons grated Parmesan
  cheese

Cook lobster tails, remove meat and cut into ½" pieces. Melt butter in a saucepan and sauté celery until soft. Stir in flour and salt. Remove from heat. Gradually add milk. Return to stove and cook over medium heat, stirring constantly, until thickened. Cook 2 additional minutes. Add small amount of hot mixture to beaten egg. Slowly pour beaten egg into saucepan, and cook an additional minute. Stir in yogurt, lobster, mushrooms, lemon rind, mustard, and Parmesan cheese. Heat, but do not boil. Serve over buttered toast.
Yield: 4 to 6 servings.

KING CRAB CASSEROLE

¾ pound king crab meat
1 cup uncooked rice
2 tablespoons butter
½ cup chopped celery
¼ cup chopped green pepper
¼ cup chopped onion
1 10½-oz. can condensed cream of
  mushroom soup

1 cup grated Cheddar cheese
1 cup yogurt
¼ cup pimento
½ teaspoon salt
⅛ teaspoon Worcestershire sauce

Cook, drain and flake crab meat. Cook rice according to package directions. Melt butter in a large skillet and sauté celery, green pepper, and onion 5 minutes. Remove from heat and add soup, Cheddar cheese, yogurt, pimento, salt, and Worcestershire sauce. In a baking dish, layer rice and crab meat. Pour sauce over all. Bake 30 minutes at 350°.
Yield: 6 to 8 servings.

SALMON BAKE*

4 salmon steaks, about 1½ pounds
  in all

2 teaspoons grated lemon rind
1 teaspoon salt

1 cup yogurt
1½ tablespoons flour
1 tablespoon finely chopped onion

⅛ teaspoon paprika
4 drops Tabasco sauce

Place salmon steaks in a shallow, buttered baking dish. Combine remaining ingredients and pour over salmon steaks. Bake at 350° for 30 minutes. *Yield: 4 servings.*

*A low-calorie dish: approximately 340 calories per serving.

SHRIMP OVER RICE

3 tablespoons butter
½ cup chopped onion
1 small clove garlic, minced
¼ cup all-purpose flour
1 teaspoon salt
½ teaspoon dry dill weed

1 10½-oz. can beef broth
1 2-oz. can mushrooms
2 cups cooked shrimp
1 cup yogurt
1 cup rice

Melt butter in a large skillet and lightly sauté onion and garlic until soft. Add flour, salt, dill weed. Stir. Remove from heat. Gradually stir in beef broth and mushrooms. Cook over medium heat until thickened. Stir constantly. Turn heat to low and add shrimp. Cook 5 to 10 minutes longer. Blend in yogurt. Heat, but do not boil. Cook rice according to package directions. Serve shrimp mixture over rice.
Yield: 4 to 6 servings.

TUNA AND POTATO BAKE

3 medium potatoes, peeled and
   thinly sliced
1 7-oz. can tuna, drained and flaked
2 medium onions, thinly sliced
1 10½-oz. can condensed cream of
   mushroom soup

1 cup yogurt
1½ tablespoons flour
½ teaspoon salt
1 cup grated Cheddar cheese

Butter a shallow baking dish, and in it alternate layers of potatoes, tuna, and onions. In a mixing bowl, combine soup, yogurt, flour, and salt. Pour mixture over layered ingredients. Bake at 350° 1 hour and 25 minutes or until potatoes are cooked. Sprinkle cheese on top and bake 5 minutes longer.
Yield: 6 servings.

SCALLOPS DIVINE

3 tablespoons butter
1 small onion, chopped
1½ pounds scallops
1 2-oz. can mushrooms, drained
¼ teaspoon dried thyme
¼ teaspoon dried marjoram
¼ teaspoon pepper
2 tablespoons flour

1 cup yogurt
Salt and pepper to taste
4 cups cooked and drained elbow
  macaroni
3 tablespoons grated Parmesan cheese
3 tablespoons Italian style bread
  crumbs

In a sauce pan, melt 1½ tablespoons butter. Add onions and sauté until soft. Add scallops, mushrooms, thyme, marjoram, and pepper. Continue cooking for 5 more minutes, or until scallops look firm. Remove from heat. Stir in flour. Fold in yogurt and mix to blend. Continue cooking over medium heat, stirring constantly, until mixture bubbles and thickens. Season with salt and pepper. Spread cooked macaroni in a 2-quart casserole. Cover with the scallop mixture. In a sauce pan, melt remaining butter. Remove from heat, and add Parmesan cheese and bread crumbs. Sprinkle mixture over casserole. Broil for a few minutes or until lightly browned. Serve at once.
Yield: 6 to 8 servings.

MEATLESS MAIN DISHES AND VEGETABLES

Yogurt is a good source for the cook who wants to prepare tasty meatless dishes. To provide something out of the ordinary in the line of vegetables, accompany meatless meals with side dishes of fresh, green, or yellow vegetables prepared with yogurt.

Many of the recipes that follow bear familiar names, but they provide a lively dash of unfamiliar enjoyment, thanks to the magic of yogurt.

BROILED YOGURT TOAST

2 cups yogurt
¼ teaspoon salt
1 small onion, finely chopped

1½ teaspoons fresh chopped parsley
8 slices whole-wheat or white bread
2 tablespoons butter, melted

Preheat broiler. Broil one side of bread only, about 3 minutes or until golden.

Combine yogurt, salt, onion, and parsley. Spread yogurt mixture on untoasted sides of bread. Sprinkle with melted butter. Broil until crisp and brown.
Yield: 4-6 servings.

CHEESE BLINTZES

1½ cups all-purpose flour
1 teaspoon salt
1¼ cups water
4 eggs

⅔ cup milk
Butter
1 cup yogurt

Filling:
1 pound cottage cheese
1 egg
1 tablespoon sugar

Sift flour and salt. Add water and mix until fairly smooth. Add eggs and beat well. Add milk and mix to a thin batter. In a 6 in. skillet, heat a small amount of butter. Pour in ¼ cup batter. Cook slowly until pancake is lightly browned on bottom and set on top. Turn. Repeat, making about 12 pancakes. Combine ingredients for filling. Place an equal amount of cheese filling in center of each pancake. Fold in ends and roll. Brown pancakes in small amount of butter. Serve topped with yogurt.
Yield: 4 servings.

MACARONI CASSEROLE

1 cup uncooked elbow macaroni
2 medium onions, chopped
2 tablespoons butter
1½ cups large curd cottage cheese

½ cup yogurt
1 egg, well beaten
2 tablespoons crushed corn flakes

Cook macaroni according to package. Drain. Cool. Sauté onions in butter until soft. Combine macaroni, onions, cottage cheese, yogurt, and egg. Pour into a buttered 1-quart casserole. Top with corn flakes, and bake at 350° for 25 to 30 minutes.
Yield: 4 servings.

GREEN SPEARS AND EGGS*

1½ pounds fresh asparagus	1 teaspoon chopped fresh dill
4 hard-boiled eggs, sliced	1 teaspoon chopped fresh parsley
2 egg yolks	Salt to taste
1 cup yogurt	Parsley for garnish
1 teaspoon lemon juice	

Break off asparagus stalks as far down as they snap easily. Wash well. Cook covered in 1-inch boiling salted water 10 to 20 minutes or until tender. Drain. Place on serving dish. Arrange egg slices on top of asparagus. Beat egg yolks in top part of double boiler. Add yogurt and lemon juice. Heat until thick and smooth. Add dill, parsley, and salt. Cool before spooning over asparagus. Garnish with parsley.
Yield: 4 to 6 servings.

*A low-calorie dish: approximately 185 calories per serving.

SCRAMBLED EGGS

6 eggs	½ teaspoon salt
½ cup plain or orange yogurt	2 tablespoons butter

In a mixing bowl, combine eggs, yogurt, and salt. Beat until just blended. Melt butter in a frying pan over low heat. Add egg mixture. As eggs begin to thicken, turn with a spatula. Do not stir, do not overcook.
Yield: 2 to 4 servings.

SPINACH AND RICE

1 pound fresh spinach	½ cup uncooked rice
¼ cup olive oil	1 8-oz. can tomato sauce
1 medium onion, chopped	Salt and pepper to taste
1½ cups hot water	1½ cups yogurt
1 tablespoon chopped fresh parsley	

Wash spinach thoroughly and drain. In a large pot, heat oil and sauté onion until golden. Add spinach and water to onion and bring to a boil. Reduce heat to simmer. Add parsley, rice, and tomato sauce and stir. Season to taste. Cover and cook until rice is done, about 20 minutes. Add more water if necessary. Serve with yogurt.
Yield: 4 to 6 servings.

TOP-NOTCH EGGS AND MUSHROOMS

½ pound fresh mushrooms, cleaned
  and cut in slices
4 tablespoons butter
8 hard-cooked eggs, quartered
  lengthwise
1 17-oz. can peas, drained
1 8-oz. can water chestnuts,
  drained and sliced
1 10½-oz. can condensed cream
  of celery soup

1 cup yogurt
¼ cup milk
1 teaspoon instant, minced onion
¼ cup sherry
3 tablespoons chopped pimento
  (optional)
Salt and pepper to taste
1 cup bread crumbs

Preheat oven to 375°. Sauté mushrooms in 2 tablespoons of the butter. In a greased 2½-quart baking dish, place mushrooms, egg quarters, peas, and water chestnuts. In a saucepan, combine soup, yogurt, milk, and onion. Heat over low flame. Remove from heat and stir in sherry, pimento, salt, and pepper. Pour over ingredients in baking dish. Melt remaining 2 tablespoons butter. Mix with bread crumbs and sprinkle over all. Bake 20 minutes or until hot and bubbly.
Yield: 8 servings.

WATER CHESTNUT SOUFFLE

5 egg yolks
1 cup yogurt
5 egg whites

1 8-oz. can water chestnuts, chopped
Salt and pepper to taste

Beat egg yolks lightly until combined. Fold in yogurt. Beat egg whites until stiff then carefully fold into yolk-yogurt mixture. Add water chestnuts and seasonings. Turn into a buttered 1½-quart souffle mold and bake 20 minutes at 375°.
Yield: 4 servings.

BROILED TOMATOES*

4 fresh tomatoes
½ cup yogurt
½ cup bread crumbs
¼ cup grated Romano cheese

¼ teaspoon oregano
¼ teaspoon garlic salt
1 teaspoon fresh chopped parsley
Salt and pepper to taste

Preheat broiler. Cut tomatoes in half. Combine remaining ingredients and spread over tomatoes. Broil about 5 minutes, or until tops are golden.
Yield: 8 servings.

*A low-calorie dish: approximately 65 calories per serving.

CAULIFLOWER AND PEAS

1 cup cauliflower, cut in small
    pieces
1¼ cups fresh peas
¼ teaspoon salt

Water
1 cup yogurt
¼ teaspoon powdered cumin
½ teaspoon salt

Cover cauliflower and peas with salted water. Cook until tender. Drain. Refrigerate. Combine yogurt, salt, and cumin. Mix with vegetables.
Yield: 4-6 servings.

FRIED CARROTS

6 medium carrots
¼ teaspoon salt
1 egg, beaten
½ cup Italian style bread crumbs

2 tablespoons butter
½ cup yogurt
¼ teaspoon salt

Wash and scrape carrots. Cut in thick strips. Place in a pan, cover with water, add salt, and cook for 10 minutes. Drain. Dip carrots in beaten egg, then roll in bread crumbs to coat. In a large skillet, melt butter over medium heat. Fry carrots until bread crumbs turn golden brown. Place on serving dish and keep warm. Combine yogurt and salt. Pour over carrots. Serve immediately.
Yield: 4 servings.

HUNGARIAN CAULIFLOWER*

1 medium-sized cauliflower
1½ cups yogurt
1 teaspoon onion salt

1 teaspoon parsley flakes
3 tablespoons bread crumbs

Cut off hard stem and remove leaves from cauliflower. Wash and break into flowerets. Place them, uncovered, in about 1-inch boiling unsalted water. Reduce heat to simmer, partially cover and cook until just tender, about 15 minutes. Drain. Combine yogurt, onion salt, and parsley flakes. Place flowerets in baking dish. Pour yogurt mixture over all. Sprinkle with bread crumbs and bake at 425° for 5 minutes.
Yield: 4 to 6 servings.

*A low-calorie dish: approximately 135 calories per serving.

ONIONS AND YOGURT

2 medium onions, thinly sliced
½ teaspoon salt
⅓ cup sugar

½ cup unsweetened grated coconut
1 cup yogurt

In a mixing bowl, combine onions and salt. Set aside for 30 minutes. Drain and squeeze out any moisture. Add sugar, coconut, and yogurt to onions. Mix well.
Yield: 4 servings.

SQUASH WITH YOGURT SAUCE

1 cup all-purpose flour
½ teaspoon baking soda
1½ teaspoons salt
1 egg
½ cup water

3 medium summer squash
Oil for deep frying
½ garlic clove, minced
2 cups yogurt

Combine flour, baking soda, and ½ teaspoon of the salt. Beat egg with water. Stir into flour mixture to make a medium batter. Heat oil for frying. Peel squash and cut into thin slices. Dip slices into batter and fry until golden brown. Drain on absorbent paper. Keep warm. Combine garlic, yogurt and remaining teaspoon salt. Spread over squash and serve.
Yield: 6 servings.

YOGURT STUFFED POTATOES*

2 large baking potatoes
¼ cup yogurt
¼ cup cottage cheese

2 tablespoons chopped fresh parsley
Salt and pepper to taste

Bake potatoes until done. Cut into halves horizontally. Remove potato pulp, being careful to keep skins intact. Mash pulp. Add yogurt, cheese, parsley, and seasonings. Fill potato shells. Reheat in 450° oven about 10 minutes.
Yield: 4 servings.

*A low-calorie dish: approximately 110 calories per serving.

DESSERTS AND BEVERAGES

Astonish yourself—not to mention your family and guests—by using yogurt in the preparation of unusual desserts and sweet snacks.

For a simple light dessert, for example, you can try spooning yogurt over fresh or canned fruit. And for a real treat or that special occasion, grace your table with an exotic yogurt cake.

You can also use fruit-flavored yogurt as a topping on plain, pound, or angel cake, or over vanilla ice cream to make a sundae. Why not give our traditional pumpkin pie a new twist by topping it with orange yogurt?

Yogurt in any flavor can serve as the base for a wide range of refreshing beverages. It is versatile enough to be mixed into milk shakes, or using your favorite sherbert, into a novel refreshing drink.

At breakfast time, yogurt blends beautifully with tomato, pineapple, or prune juice—a good way for anyone to start the day.

APRICOT PARFAIT

1 cup apricot-flavored yogurt
½ cup chopped dried dates
2 tablespoons honey

1 teaspoon lemon juice
½ teaspoon cinnamon
Shredded coconut for garnish

Combine all ingredients except coconut. Spoon into parfait glasses and garnish with coconut.
Yield: 6 servings.

BANANA CREPES

½ cup sifted cake flour
2 teaspoons sugar
½ teaspoon salt
2 cups milk
2 eggs
Butter

1 cup pineapple flavored yogurt
2 bananas peeled and sliced
½ cup flaked coconut
1 teaspoon rum extract
Confectioners' sugar

Sift flour, sugar, and salt into a bowl. Add milk and eggs and beat until smooth. In an 8-inch skillet, melt a small amount of butter. Pour ¼ cup batter into skillet,

tilting pan immediately so batter will cover entire bottom. Cook crepe on both sides until light brown. Remove and roll up immediately. Keep warm. Continue until all batter is used, adding butter to skillet as necessary. Combine yogurt, bananas, coconut, and rum extract. Unroll crepes and divide yogurt mixture among them. Reroll. Sprinkle with sugar.
Yield: about 12 crepes.

BLUEBERRY TORTE

2¼ cups crushed chocolate wafers
½ cup butter
2 cups confectioners' sugar
2 eggs
2 teaspoons lemon juice
1 teaspoon grated lemon rind
¾ cup chopped walnuts
2 cups whipping cream
2 cups blueberry-flavored yogurt

In a 9 x 9-inch baking dish, spread 1½ cups of the wafers and pack them down. In a mixing bowl, cream butter with confectioners' sugar. Add eggs and beat thoroughly. Add lemon juice and lemon rind. Beat to a smooth, creamy consistency. Pour mixture over wafers and spread evenly, taking care to keep creamed mixture from intermixing with wafers. Sprinkle walnuts over mixture. Whip cream until it forms peaks. Blend in yogurt. Cover nuts with cream-yogurt mixture. Top with remaining wafers. Refrigerate at least 2 hours before serving.
Yield: 6 to 8 servings.

CHERRY BREAD PUDDING

12 slices white bread
Butter
Cinnamon
1 cup cherry preserves
4 eggs
2⅔ cups milk
2 tablespoons granulated sugar
1½ cups cherry-flavored or plain yogurt

Preheat oven to 325°. Cut crusts from bread. Butter one side of each slice. Butter an 8 x 8 baking dish. Place 4 slices of bread, buttered side up, in bottom of dish. Sprinkle lightly with cinnamon. Spread a spoonful of cherry preserves on each slice. Repeat, making two more layers. In a bowl, beat eggs. Add milk and sugar, stirring until well mixed. Pour over bread and bake 1 hour. Serve warm or at room temperature, topped with yogurt.
Yield: 6 servings.

CHOCOLATE CHIP COOKIES

½ cup butter
1½ cups brown sugar
2 eggs
1 teaspoon vanilla extract
2½ cups all-purpose flour
1 teaspoon baking soda
½ teaspoon baking powder
½ teaspoon salt
1 cup yogurt
1 12-oz. package semisweet
    chocolate pieces
1 cup chopped walnuts (optional)

Preheat oven to 375°. Cream butter in a mixing bowl. Gradually add sugar and beat until light and fluffy. Add eggs and vanilla and beat until well blended. Sift together flour, baking soda, baking powder, and salt. Alternately add yogurt and dry ingredients to butter mixture. Begin and end with dry ingredients. Add chocolate pieces and chopped nuts. Drop by rounded teaspoonfuls onto greased cookie sheets. Bake 10-12 minutes. Remove immediately to wire rack and allow to cool.
Yield: about 4 dozen.

DELECTABLE CHIFFON PIE

2 tablespoons unflavored gelatin
½ cup sugar
1 cup water
¾ cup orange juice
2 cups yogurt
2 egg whites
2 tablespoons sugar

Pie crust:
1⅓ cups graham crackers
2 tablespoons sugar
¼ cup melted butter

In a saucepan, combine gelatin, ½ cup sugar, and water. Stir over low heat until gelatin is dissolved. Combine orange juice and yogurt. Stir gelatin mixture into yogurt mixture and chill until nearly set. Beat egg whites until frothy. Gradually add sugar to egg whites and beat until stiff. Fold into orange mixture, and refrigerate until it begins to set. Turn into pie crust. Chill until set.
Yield: 8 servings.

Pie crust:
Crumble graham crackers and mix with sugar. Melt butter and combine with crackers. Press mixture firmly in an even layer against bottom and sides of a 9-inch pie pan. Chill before using.

FROZEN ORANGE-COCONUT TREAT

1 egg white	¼ teaspoon vanilla extract
½ pint whipping cream	1 cup orange-flavored yogurt
2 tablespoons sugar	1 cup toasted, shredded coconut

In a bowl, beat egg white, cream, sugar, and vanilla until stiff peaks form. Fold in yogurt and toasted coconut. Spoon mixture into 3-oz. paper cups and freeze until firm, about 2 to 3 hours.
Yield: 4 to 6 servings.

LEMON FROTH*

1 6-oz. can lemonade (or limeade) frozen concentrate	½ cup sugar
	1 cup yogurt
1 tablespoon unflavored gelatin	2 egg whites

Thaw lemonade. Combine gelatin and ½ cup of the lemonade. Heat over low flame until gelatin dissolves. Away from heat, add sugar and stir until dissolved. Blend in yogurt and remaining lemonade. Chill. Stir occasionally. When mixture mounds slightly when dropped from spoon, add egg whites. With electric beater set at high, beat mixture 5 to 7 minutes until it is light and has doubled in volume. Spoon into serving dishes and chill at least 2 hours.
Yield: 4 servings.

*A low-calorie dessert: approximately 180 calories per serving.

MOCHA MOLD

1 3-oz. package chocolate pudding and pie filling	2½ cups milk
	1 cup cottage cheese
1 tablespoon unflavored gelatin	¼ cup sugar
2 teaspoons instant coffee	½ cup vanilla-flavored yogurt
2 eggs, separated	

In a saucepan, combine pudding, gelatin, coffee, and egg yolks. Stir in milk. Set over medium heat and cook until mixture comes to a boil and thickens. Cool. Whirl cottage cheese in blender. Add to gelatin mixture and beat in. Refrigerate until mixture mounds on a spoon. Beat egg whites until frothy. Gradually add sugar to egg whites, beating until peaks form. Fold into gelatin mixture. Fold in yogurt. Pour mixture into greased 6-cup ring mold. Chill until firm.
Yield: 8 servings.

MOM'S DELICIOUS YOGURT CAKE

1 cup sweet butter
2½ cups sugar
  5 eggs, well beaten
  1 cup yogurt
 ½ teaspoon baking soda

½ cup milk
 3 cups sifted cake flour
 3 teaspoons baking powder
 1 cup finely chopped walnuts

Syrup:
1½ cups sugar
2½ cups water

Preheat oven to 325°. Melt butter. Cool. Gradually add sugar to butter. Cream together thoroughly. Add eggs and mix well. Blend in yogurt. In a mixing bowl, combine soda and milk. Add to mixture. Combine flour and baking powder and blend, one cup at a time, into the yogurt mixture. Beat batter until thoroughly blended. Pour batter into a greased 13 x 9-inch baking pan and bake for 60 minutes, or until medium brown. The top should spring back when pressed lightly. While cake is still hot, cut into serving pieces. Sprinkle with chopped walnuts. Slowly spoon cooled syrup over hot cake.
Yield: 10 to 12 servings.

Syrup:
Combine sugar and water in a saucepan. Boil gently about 25 minutes. Remove from heat. Cool.

PARTY CHOCOLATE CAKE

½ cup water
 3 1-oz. squares unsweetened
   chocolate
 1 cup yogurt
½ cup butter
 1 cup granulated sugar

½ cup brown sugar
 3 eggs
 1 teaspoon vanilla extract
 2 cups sifted cake flour
 1 teaspoon baking soda
 1 teaspoon salt

Chocolate Glaze:
 1 6-oz. package semisweet chocolate
½ cup yogurt

Preheat oven to 350°. Place water and chocolate in a saucepan. Set over low heat until chocolate melts. Stir constantly. Set aside to cool. Add yogurt to cooled chocolate. In a mixing bowl, cream butter. Slowly add both kinds of sugar and

beat until light and fluffy. Beat in eggs, one at a time. Add vanilla. Sift together flour, soda, and salt. Add dry ingredients to creamed mixture alternately with yogurt mixture. Begin and end with dry ingredients. Butter a 13 x 9 x 2-inch pan and dust with flour. Pour in batter. Bake 35 to 40 minutes. Cool. Spread chocolate glaze on top.
Yield: about 12 servings.

Chocolate Glaze:
Melt chocolate pieces over low heat. Stir constantly. Remove from heat. Blend in yogurt. Cool.

PEAR NUT SQUARES

¼ cup butter
¼ cup firmly packed light brown
   sugar
1 egg
½ teaspoon vanilla extract
1 cup all-purpose flour
2 eggs, beaten

1 cup yogurt
½ cup sugar
¼ teaspoon nutmeg
¼ teaspoon ground ginger
¼ cup chopped walnuts
1 1-pound can pear halves, drained
   and sliced

Preheat oven to 325°. In a mixing bowl, cream butter, add brown sugar, and beat until fluffy and light. Beat in egg and vanilla. Gradually add flour and mix until blended. Pour batter into a 8-inch square cake pan. Bake 15 minutes. Mix eggs, yogurt, sugar, nutmeg, and ginger thoroughly. Add walnuts. Arrange sliced pears on the cake. Pour custard over pears. Bake 45-50 minutes longer. Test for readiness by inserting a knife in center of custard. If blade comes out clean, remove pan from oven. Serve warm.
Yield: 8 to 10 servings.

PINEAPPLE CREAM PUFFS

2 cups whipping cream
¼ cup sugar
½ teaspoon salt

½ teaspoon vanilla extract
2 cups pineapple-flavored yogurt
Confectioners' sugar

Cream puffs:
1 cup water
½ cup butter

1 cup sifted all-purpose flour
4 eggs

In a chilled bowl, combine cream, sugar, salt, and vanilla, and whip. Fold in yogurt. Spoon mixture into cream puffs and chill. Before serving, dust with confectioners' sugar.

Cream puffs:
Preheat oven to 400°. Bring water and butter to a rolling boil. Stir in flour all at once. Stir vigorously over low heat until mixture leaves sides of pan and forms a ball (about 1 minute). Remove from heat. Add eggs, one at a time, beating thoroughly after each addition. Beat again until smooth and velvety. Drop from spoon onto ungreased baking sheet 3'' apart. Bake 45-50 minutes, or until puffed and golden brown. Cool away from drafts.
Yield: 8 puffs.

SESAME DOUGHNUTS

2 cups yogurt	2¾ cups all-purpose flour
4 teaspoons grated orange rind	Vegetable oil for frying
1 tablespoon orange juice	Sesame seeds
¼ teaspoon salt	Cinnamon
1 teaspoon baking powder	

Syrup:
 1 cup honey
½ cup water
 3 tablespoons sugar

In a large bowl, combine yogurt, orange rind, juice, salt, and baking powder. Gradually stir in flour. Cover bowl with a kitchen towel and set in a warm place for 1 hour. Heat at least 3 inches of vegetable oil in a heavy pan. Drop batter into hot oil by the teaspoonful, wetting spoon after each use so batter will not stick. Fry a few at a time until golden brown, turning when edges show darker color. Drain on absorbent paper. Dip warm doughnuts in warm syrup, then roll in sesame seeds. Sprinkle with cinnamon.
Yield: 3 dozen doughnuts.
Syrup:
Boil honey, water, and sugar together for 5 minutes.

VIENNA RIPPLE

2 3-oz. packages mixed-fruit gelatin	¼ cup kirsch
2 cups boiling water	2 cups raspberry-flavored yogurt
2 cups cold water	

Dissolve gelatin in 2 cups boiling water. Stir in 2 cups cold water and kirsch. Apportion one cup of mixture evenly into 8 parfait glasses. Refrigerate until firm. Refrigerate remaining gelatin in a bowl until set, then place bowl in another bowl containing crushed ice. With an electric mixer, beat gelatin until light and foamy. Gently stir yogurt, then fold into beaten gelatin. Spoon mixture into parfait glasses. Refrigerate until firm.
Yield: 8 servings.

WALNUT CAKE

½ cup ground walnuts	½ cup butter
½ cup fine sugar	2 cups flour
1 teaspoon cinnamon	1½ teaspoons baking powder
2 eggs	1 teaspoon baking soda
1 cup granulated sugar	1 cup yogurt

Preheat oven to 350°. Mix first 3 ingredients and set aside. Beat together eggs, granulated sugar, and butter for 3 minutes. Sift together flour, baking powder, and soda. Add to butter mixture. Add yogurt to batter. Mix well. Pour half the batter into a greased 9 x 9-inch cake pan. Spoon half of the walnut mixture over it. Repeat with remaining batter and walnuts. Bake 30 minutes, then reduce heat to 300° and bake 10 minutes longer.
Yield: 8 to 10 servings.

YOGURT POPSICLES

2 cups fruit-flavored yogurt

Mix, if necessary, to distribute fruit evenly

or

2 cups plain yogurt   *
½ cup fruit juice
1 teaspoon vanilla extract

Combine ingredients

or

2 cups plain yogurt
6 teaspoons jam or preserves

Combine ingredients

Divide yogurt into 6 3-oz. paper cups. Insert a wooden stick or plastic spoon in

center of each cup. Freeze. To eat, peel off paper covering.
Yield: 6 servings.

*Low-calorie popsicles: approximately 60 calories per serving.

BEVERAGES

Orange Refresher
  2 cups orange sherbet
  2 cups yogurt
½ cup fresh orange juice

Pineapple Frosted
  2 cups vanilla-flavored yogurt
  1 cup pineapple sherbet
½ cup pineapple juice

Sherbet Cooler
  2 cups lime sherbet
  2 cups raspberry-flavored yogurt
½ cup cranberry juice

Prune Nectar
  2 cups prune juice
  2 cups yogurt
Dash of cinnamon
  1 tablespoon lemon juice
  2 tablespoons honey

*Tomato-Yogurt Juice**
  2 cups yogurt
  2 cups tomato juice
  2 teaspoons lemon juice
Dash of salt

Vanilla Milk Shake
  2 cups vanilla-flavored yogurt
  2 cups skim milk
  2 tablespoons sugar

Place ingredients in blender and mix thoroughly at low speed. Serve in tall frosted glasses.
Yield: 3 to 4 servings.

*A low-calorie drink: approximately 90 calories per serving.

BREADS

Bread has such an immensely long history as a staple food that it is hard to imagine some new way of making it. Yogurt, too, has played an age-old role in nourishing mankind, but we seldom think of using the two together. Yet, the addition of yogurt to bread, biscuits, and pancake recipes contributes a light texture and a piquant flavor that few ingredients can match.

BANANA-NUT BREAD

1½ cups all-purpose flour	⅓ cup salad oil
1 teaspoon salt	2 eggs, slightly beaten
2 teaspoons baking powder	⅓ cup yogurt
½ teaspoon baking soda	⅔ cup mashed bananas
½ cup sugar	½ cup chopped walnuts
¾ cup rolled oats	

Preheat oven to 350°. Sift together flour, salt, baking powder, baking soda, and sugar. Stir in oats. Mix salad oil, eggs, and yogurt. Add to dry ingredients to form batter. Combine banana and nuts and stir in only until blended. Pour batter into a greased 1-pound loaf pan. Bake 50-60 minutes.
Yield: 8 to 10 servings.

BLUEBERRY MUFFINS

2 cups biscuit mix	¼ cup butter, melted
¼ cup sugar	1 egg
½ teaspoon baking soda	1 cup blueberry-flavored yogurt

Preheat oven to 400°. Combine biscuit mix, sugar, and baking soda until well blended. Add butter, egg, and yogurt. Combine liquid and dry ingredients and mix to the consistency of soft dough. Fill well-greased muffin cups ⅔ full. Bake 15 to 20 minutes.
Yield: 12 muffins.

CHEESE BREAD

1 cup yogurt	1 package active dry yeast
1 cup water	½ teaspoon baking soda
⅓ cup butter	1 cup grated medium sharp
¼ cup sugar	Cheddar cheese
1½ teaspoons salt	5 to 5½ cups all-purpose flour

Heat yogurt and water with butter until butter melts. Stir in sugar and salt and cool to about 120°F. In a large bowl, combine yeast, baking soda, and cheese with half the flour. Add yogurt mixture and beat at low speed ½ minute, then on medium-high speed 3 minutes. With a wooden spoon, stir in enough additional flour to make a soft but firm dough. Turn out on floured board and knead 7 to 10 minutes, or until smooth and elastic. Place in greased bowl and then turn the dough greased side up. Cover and let rise in warm place 1 hour, or until doubled. Punch down and shape in 2 loaves. Put in greased 9 x 5 x 3-inch loaf pan and let rise 30 to 40 minutes, or until doubled again. Preheat oven to 400°. Bake 30 to 40 minutes. Turn out on cake racks and allow to cool before cutting.
Yield: 2 medium-sized loaves.

DROP BISCUITS

1½ cups all-purpose flour	¼ teaspoon salt
2 tablespoons sugar	¼ cup butter
2 teaspoons baking powder	1 cup yogurt
¼ teaspoon baking soda	

Preheat oven to 450°. Sift together flour, sugar, baking powder, baking soda, and salt. Cut in butter with pastry blender until mixture resembles coarse meal. Add yogurt and stir only until dry ingredients are moist enough to form a dough. Drop onto a baking sheet in 6 heaping tablespoonfuls. Brush tops with water. Bake 10-15 minutes.
Yield: 6 biscuits.

EAST INDIAN BREAD

2½ cups whole-wheat flour	1⅓ cup yogurt
1¼ teaspoon salt	Oil for frying
½ cup butter	

In a mixing bowl, combine flour and salt. With a pastry blender, cut in butter

until it forms particles the size of large peas. Add yogurt and mix until well blended. Roll out dough until it is about 1/8" thick. Flour a round cookie cutter, at least 4" in diameter, and cut dough in circles. In a heavy skillet, heat at least 1 inch of oil. Fry circles until light brown and puffy. Place on absorbent paper to drain. Serve warm.
Yield: 35 to 40 pieces.

PANCAKES

3 tablespoons sugar	1 teaspoon baking powder
½ teaspoon salt	1 teaspoon baking soda
2 cups yogurt	2 cups flour
3 eggs, separated	¼ teaspoon cinnamon

In a mixing bowl, combine sugar, salt, and yogurt. Set aside. Beat egg yolks until light and thick. Sift together baking powder, baking soda, flour, and cinnamon. Combine yogurt-sugar mixture with egg yolks. Combine dry ingredients with egg mixture and stir until smooth. Beat egg whites until stiff, but not dry. Fold egg whites into batter. Drop batter by the tablespoon on hot greased griddle, turning to brown on both sides.
Yield: 6 to 8 servings.

WHOLE WHEAT BISCUITS

1¾ cups whole wheat flour	½ teaspoon salt
4 teaspoons baking powder	⅓ cup peanut oil
¼ cup instant milk powder	¾ cup yogurt

Preheat oven to 450°. In a mixing bowl, mix flour, baking powder, milk powder, and salt. Add oil and cut in with pastry blender until mixture resembles coarse meal. Make a medium-sized hole in batter, pour in yogurt, and mix quickly. Knead lightly 10 to 15 times, using as much extra flour as necessary to hold mixture together. Roll out to ½ inch thickness and cut with floured biscuit cutter. Bake 12-15 minutes.
Yield: about 24 biscuits.

YOGURT CORN BREAD

2 eggs	⅔ cup cornmeal
¼ cup sugar	½ teaspoon salt

1 cup flour
2 teaspoons baking powder
½ teaspoon baking soda

1 cup yogurt
¼ cup butter, melted

Preheat oven to 400°. In a mixing bowl, beat eggs. Add sugar and blend well. Sift together flour, baking powder, baking soda, cornmeal, and salt. Add yogurt alternately with dry ingredients to egg-sugar mixture. Blend in butter. Pour batter into a greased 8-inch square baking pan. Bake 25 minutes.
Yield: 8-10 servings.

YOGURT CORN MUFFINS

Proceed as in recipe for Corn Bread, using same ingredients and repeating first six steps. Then: fill 12 greased muffin cups ⅔ full. Bake 25 minutes.
Yield: 12 muffins.

CHEESE

No matter what conditions
Dyspeptic come to feaze,
The best of all physicians
Is apple-pie and cheese!

Eugene Field

CHEESE

Cheese, unlike its ancient cousin, yogurt, is not a novel food to Americans. It came over to America with the earliest settlers who made Cheddar cheese in their own homes.

Like yogurt, though, the popularity of cheese has been steadily growing. One of the most natural and oldest of food products, dating back to the domestication of animals, about 9000 B.C., cheese was once so highly esteemed it was even used as a medium of exchange. It traveled with the Greeks, the Romans and with the armies of Genghis Khan. During the Middle Ages, monks in the French monasteries developed a soft-ripened cheese, starting a cheese renaissance. Centuries later, in 1851, Jesse Williams built the first commercial cheese factory in America. Herkimer, in upstate New York, grew into the cheese center of the United States until the westward expansion of the country resulted in Wisconsin gradually exceeding New York in total annual production. As pioneer wagons moved west, boats continued to carry others from across the ocean. The immigrants introduced their own favorite cheeses to America and contributed to the "melting (cheese) pot."

As the number of cheeses available in the United States has enlarged, so has the consumer demand. The consumption of cheese in 1975 was 14.2 pounds per person compared to 9.1 pounds in 1965.

We all have a favorite cheese. Mine is sharp Parmesan. I remember buying it by the pound for my mother at the local delicatessen where real (not plastic) provolones hung from the ceiling. I would take the Parmesan home and help to grate it just before she would sprinkle it on piping hot spaghetti covered with melted, browned butter.

The hardest cheese I have ever eaten, and I mean a hard cheese, was served to me by the good people of Hedera, on the Island of Mytilene in the Aegean Sea, the village from which my father emigrated. The cheese, made from goat's milk, wasn't feta or kasseri, or any known Greek type, but the villagers' own prized cheese. For me it wasn't quite eatable, but eat it I did, and as I ate I could feel the centuries of cheese-making compressed into its hard grain.

When I shop for cheese I sometimes remember that humble goat cheese as I scan the enormous selection from which I have to choose. It's been estimated that there are from 400 to 2000 different kinds. Sometimes it is difficult to sort one's way through the abundance without a guide. I have found a simple method of cheese classification that can help reduce the confusion. I start by dividing all the cheeses of the world into just two categories: *natural* and *processed*. Following is a breakdown of these two major cheese categories which will give you a quick comparison of familiar cheeses.

NATURAL CHEESES

Natural cheese is a product of milk that has been heated, pressed, and cured. In the United States, cheese is made from pasteurized cow's milk. Whole milk is generally used except for some varieties such as cottage cheese which uses skim milk. When milk is heated, usually with a starter of some kind (rennet or bacterial culture), it separates into a soft curd and a liquid whey.

After the milk has been heated, but before it has started to ripen, the soft curd may be separated from the whey and with some additional treatment made into a fresh natural *unripened* cheese.

Following are the main examples of the *unripened* cheeses.

NATURAL UNRIPENED CHEESES

Unripened cheeses contain relatively high moisture and do not undergo any curing or ripening. They are sold fresh and should be used within a few days after purchase. The gjetost and primost, however, because they contain very low moisture, may be kept refrigerated for several weeks or even months.

Cottage cheese, a low calorie cheese, is made in different sized curds. The small-curd type is usually used in salads because it holds its shape better than the larger curds which are suitable for all other purposes. To prepare creamed cottage cheese, fresh cream is mixed with the curd to give it additional moisture and flavor.

Cream cheese is of American origin and is one of our most popular soft cheeses. It is a mixture of milk and cream that is coagulated but unripened. American type Neufchatel is similar to cream cheese but has a lower fat content and more moisture.

Unripened cheese may also be divided into *soft* or *firm* types.

Cream cheese and cottage cheese are examples of a *soft* unripened cheese, as are Neufchatel (domestic variety) and ricotta. Examples of *firm* unripened cheese are gjetsot, primost, and mozzarella.

This unripened cheese list also contains examples of what are known as *whey* cheeses. Whey cheeses are made from the liquid whey rather than the curd. The most familiar to us is the ricotta which today is made in a modified manner by mixing whey and whole or skim milk. Gjetsot and primost are Scandinavian *whey* cheeses to which fat has been added.

NATURAL UNRIPENED CHEESES

Type or name	Place of origin	Kind of milk used	Flavor	Uses
Cottage (plain or creamed)	Unknown	Cow's milk skimmed; plain curd or with cream added	Mild, slightly acid	Salads, dips, cooking ingredient
Cream	U.S.A.	Cream from cow's milk	Mild, slightly acid	Salads, dips, snacks, sandwiches, desserts
Gjetost (imported only)	Norway	Whey from goat's milk or mixture of goat's and cow's milk	Sweetish	Appetizers, snacks, desserts
Mozzarella	Italy	Cow's milk, whole or partly skimmed	Mild, delicate	Snacks, sandwiches, cooking ingredient
Neufchatel	France	Cow's milk	Mild	Appetizers, snacks, desserts
Primost	Norway	Whey from cow's milk	Sweetish, caramel	Appetizers, snacks, desserts
Ricotta	Italy	Cow's milk, whole or partly skimmed (In Italy, whey from sheep's milk)	Bland, but semisweet	Salads, dips, cooking ingredient

55

NATURAL RIPENED CHEESES

To make natural ripened cheese, the soft curd is taken from the liquid whey and then cured by holding it at a certain temperature and humidity for a specified period of time.

Natural ripened cheeses may also be classified according to their degree of hardness. Authorities generally group natural cheese into four distinct groups of hardness: soft, semi-soft, firm, and very hard. Hardness has to do with moisture. The older the cheese, the lower its moisture content.

Following are examples of the more important natural ripened cheeses according to level of hardness.

Soft Natural Ripened Cheeses

Brie and *Camembert*, both of which originated in France, are ripened by mold. The curd is not cut nor is it pressed. Cheese lovers all over the world hold these two cheeses in the highest of esteem.

Brie is considered to be the Queen of Cheeses. There are probably more literary references to Brie than to any other cheese. Its descriptions are often accompanied by superlatives but it is a difficult cheese to buy satisfactorily because it goes from underipened to overripened in a matter of a few days. It is at its peak when it has a consistency of a heavy slow-pouring liquid and a yellow sheen. Underripe Brie is flaky and chalky. Overripe Brie is very soft and has an off-odor like ammonia. The three French varieties are Meaux, Melun, and Coulommiers.

Camembert is a very popular cheese in France and is widely known in the United States. It has as devoted a following as Brie and also the same ephemeral quality of being ripe for only a very short time.

Limburger and *Liederkranz* are examples of bacteria-ripened cheeses. The different bacteria used in the ripening process are responsible for their characteristic flavor and odor. Limburger originated in Belgium, is also made in Germany and in the United States. It has a very strong odor but the domestic variety is not as strong.

Liederkranz originated in Monroe, New York by Emil Frey. It is not as strong a cheese as Limburger. It should be eaten when ripe, that is when its texture is soft and pliant but not runny.

SOFT NATURAL RIPENED CHEESES

The soft cheeses are cured from the outside, or rind of the cheese, inward by the action of molds or bacterial cultures which grow on the surface. Curing continues as long as the temperature is favorable. Once cut, however, its maturation process terminates. These cheeses usually contain more moisture than the other cheeses.

Type or name	Place of origin	Kind of milk used	Ripening period	Flavor	Uses
Brie	France	Cow's milk	4 to 8 weeks	Mild to pungent	Appetizers, snacks, sandwiches, desserts
Camembert	France	Cow's milk	4 to 8 weeks	Mild to pungent	Appetizers, snacks, sandwiches, desserts
Liederkranz (trade mark)	U.S.A.	Cow's milk	3 to 4 weeks	Hearty, robust	Appetizers, snacks, desserts
Limburger	Belgium	Cow's milk	4 to 8 weeks	Highly pungent, strong	Appetizers, snacks, desserts

Semi-Soft Natural Ripened Cheeses

Included in this category are the blue-veined cheeses. There are now over fifty varieties of blue cheeses made all over the world. However, the best known and most highly prized are Roquefort, Stilton, and Gorgonzola.

Blue cheeses are called the "king of cheeses." They are made from cow's milk. Roquefort is the exception. It is made from sheep's milk and is cured in the cool, damp caves of southeastern France.

Bel Paese is a popular, all purpose cheese made in Italy and under license in the United States (Wisconsin). It is a table cheese as well as a cooking cheese.

Brick is an original American cheese whose name derives from either the shape of the cheese or, perhaps, from the brick originally used in pressing the curd. It is softer than Cheddar and less sharp. It is a strong cheese, but not as strong as Limburger.

Muenster, as made in France where it is very popular, is a strong cheese. It is used as a table cheese. However, the American kind is much more bland and is suitable for cooking as well as for a table cheese.

Port du Salut originated in a Trappist monastery in France. The French import is usually mellow with a slight edge.

SEMI-SOFT NATURAL RIPENED CHEESES

Semi-soft ripened cheeses are ripened by dual action. They ripen from the interior outward as well as from the surface inward. The ripening process is performed by bacterial or mold cultures or both.

Type or name	Place of origin	Kind of milk used	Ripening period	Flavor	Uses
Bel Paese (U.S. made; also imported)	Italy	Cow's milk	6 to 8 weeks	Mild to robust	Appetizers, snacks, cooking ingredients, desserts
Blue (Bleu imported)	France	Cow's milk	2 to 6 months	Tangy, spicy	Appetizers, salads, desserts
Brick	U.S.A.	Cow's milk	2 to 4 months	Mild to moderately sharp	Appetizers, snacks, sandwiches, desserts
Gorgonzola	Italy	Cow's milk (In Italy: cow's milk, goat's milk or a mixture of both)	3 to 12 months	Tangy, spicy	Appetizers, salads, dips, sandwiches, desserts
Muenster	France	Cow's milk	1 to 8 weeks	Mild to mellow	Appetizers, snacks, sandwiches, desserts
Port du Salut	France	Cow's milk	6 to 8 weeks	Mellow to robust	Appetizers, snacks, desserts
Roquefort (Imported only)	France	Sheep's milk	2 to 5 months or more	Sharp, slightly spicy	Appetizers, salads, sandwiches, dips, desserts
Stilton (Imported only)	England	Cow's milk	2 to 6 months	Piquant, milder than Roquefort	Appetizers, snacks, salads, desserts

Firm Natural Ripened Cheeses

The hard or firm cheese list includes the two most popular cheeses in the United States, Cheddar and Swiss.

Cheddar cheese accounts for almost half of all the cheese consumed in America. It ranges from a very mild cheese to a very sharp one depending upon how long it's been aged. A versatile cheese, suitable for most cheese dishes, it melts well and is the prime ingredient of our processed cheeses.

Canadian Cheddar is imported into the United States, but English Cheddar, by law, is not. The English relative to Cheddar, the famous Cheshire is imported.

More American Cheddar cheese is made in Wisconsin than in any other state, but there are local variations such as New York State Cheddar and Vermont Cheddar on the East Coast, Colby in the Midwest, and Monterey (Jack) and Tillamook on the West Coast. Colby, not as compressed as the other Cheddars, has a higher moisture content. Monterey is also a milder Cheddar and has a higher moisture content. There is a more aged Monterey called "dry Monterey" that can be used for grating.

A large amount of Cheddar cheese made in the United States is sold as processed American cheese. Processed cheeses are not a part of these natural cheese charts. For a further discussion on processed cheese see page 62.

The distinguishing feature of *Swiss* (*Emmentaler*) and *Gruyere* are their "eyes" which develop throughout the cheeses by the action of certain bacteria forming gases. Both Swiss and Gruyere have a sweet nut-like flavor but the Gruyere has a sharper flavor, is more firm, and has much smaller "eyes." They are fine melting cheeses. The original Swiss Fondue was made from a combination of these two cheeses.

Other countries make their own version of Swiss cheese including Austria, Finland, Denmark, and the United States. Some Swiss cheeses, both imported and domestic, are sold as a processed Gruyere (or Swiss) cheese and may contain both Emmentaler and Gruyere.

Provolone and *Cacciocavalle* are spun cheeses. The curd is placed in either hot water or hot whey and then stretched into its desired shape or size. They are an important ingredient in Italian cooking. The provolone is usually smoked.

The *Edam* and *Gouda* cheeses are the most popular cheeses imported from the Netherlands. Similar in flavor, the Edam is made from partly skim milk and the Gouda from whole milk.

FIRM NATURAL RIPENED CHEESES

The amount of moisture in a firm cheese is related to the temperature and length of curing. Since these cheeses are lower in moisture than the softer cheeses their curing time usually is longer. These cheeses continue to ripen as long as the temperature is favorable.

Type or name	Place of origin	Kind of milk used	Ripening period	Flavor	Uses
Caciocavalle	Italy	Cow's milk (In Italy, cow's milk or mixture of sheep's, goat's, and cow's milk	3 to 12 months	Piquant, similar to provolone but not smoked	Appetizers, snacks, sandwiches, cooking ingredient
Cheddar	England	Cow's milk	1 to 12 months or more	Mild to very sharp	Appetizers, snacks, sandwiches, salads, cooking ingredient
Colby	U.S.A.	Cow's milk	1 to 3 months	Mild to mellow	Appetizers, snacks, sandwiches, cooking ingredient
Ecam	Netherlands	Cow's milk, whole or partly skimmed	2 to 3 months	Mellow, nutlike flavor	Appetizers, snacks, sandwiches, salads
Gouda	Netherlands	Cow's milk, whole or partly skimmed	2 to 6 months	Mellow, nutlike flavor	Appetizers, snacks, sandwiches, salads
Gruyere	Switzerland	Cow's milk	3 to 9 months	Sweet, nutlike flavor, sharper than Swiss cheese	Appetizers, snacks, sandwiches, fondue, desserts
Monterey (Jack)	U.S.A.	Cow's milk	3 weeks to 6 months or more	Mild to mellow (depending on milk used and ripening period)	Appetizers, snacks, sandwiches, cooking ingredient
Provolone	Italy	Cow's milk	2 to 12 months or more	Mellow to sharp; smoky and salty	Appetizers, snacks, sandwiches, cooking ingredient
Swiss (also called Emmentaler)	Switzerland	Cow's milk	3 to 9 months	Mellow, nutlike flavor	Sandwiches, salads, snacks, fondue

61

Very Hard Cheeses

Parmesan has a mild to sharp piquant flavor and is famous as a seasoning in cooking. It has the natural ability of enhancing the flavor of foods. The imported Italian Parmesan is a highly prized cheese and is used as a table cheese as well as for seasoning. The domestic varieties are primarily grated for seasoning and for cooking.

Romano is a sharper cheese than Parmesan. In Italy it is usually made from sheep's milk (Pecorino Romano) instead of from cow's milk. It is primarily a grating cheese but the less sharp cheese may be used as a table cheese. The domestic variety is primarily a grating cheese.

Sap Sago is a grating cheese from Switzerland to which has been added dried clover. It is made by mixing whey and skimmed cow's milk.

PROCESSED CHEESES

As the name implies, it is cheese which has undergone a processing step. A cheese may be blended with another cheese (or cheeses) or ingredients are added to a cheese to alter its quality in some way.

Following are the different types of processed cheeses.

PASTEURIZED PROCESS CHEESE

is made by grinding fresh and aged natural cheeses together then heating and stirring. An emulsifying agent is then added and the mixture is worked into a homogeneous whole. The blend may consist of one or two varieties of cheese and may contain additions of spices, fruits, vegetables, or meats. The cheese may be smoked or it may be made from smoked cheese or smoke flavor may be added. The flavor is dependent upon the type cheese used. Varieties include American, Swiss, American-Swiss, brick, Limburger, Gruyere, and Colby. The greatest quantity processed, however, is American Cheddar cheese. (The unripened cheeses such as cream or cottage cheese are not used in process cheese.) It is estimated that more than one third of the ripened cheeses made in the United States is marketed as process cheese.

VERY HARD CHEESES

Very hard cheeses, as well as the firm cheeses, are ripened by bacteria culture throughout the entire cheese. Ripening continues for as long as the temperature is favorable and the longer the ripening time the harder the cheese.

Type or name	Place of origin	Kind of milk used	Ripening period	Flavor	Uses
Parmesan	Italy	Partly skimmed cow's milk	14 months to 2 years or longer	Sharp, piquant	Grated for seasoning, cooking ingredient
Romano	Italy	Cow's milk (In Italy, sheep's milk)	5 to 12 months	Sharp, strong	Grated for seasoning, cooking ingredient
Sap Sago (Imported only)	Switzerland	Skimmed cow's milk	5 months or longer	Sharp, cloverlike taste because of the addition of dried powdered clover leaves	Grated for seasoning, mixed with butter as a spread

63

PASTEURIZED PROCESS BLENDED CHEESE

is the same as process cheese except that an *unripened* natural cheese such as cream cheese or Neufchatel cheese can be used in mixtures of two or more kinds and neither emulsifier nor acid is added.

PASTEURIZED PROCESS CHEESE FOOD

is also made the same as process cheese except that certain dairy products (cream, milk, skim milk, cheese whey, or whey albumin) may be added, providing that at least 51 percent of the weight of the finished cheese food is cheese. This results in a lower milk fat content and more moisture than in process cheese. Spices, fruits, vegetables, or meats may be added. It may also have a smoked flavor. Cheese food is milder than process cheese and melts more readily due to the higher moisture.

PASTEURIZED PROCESS CHEESE SPREAD

is made the same as process cheese food except that it contains more moisture (44 to 60 percent) and less fat (but not less than 20 percent) and is spreadable at 70°F. A stabilizer is used in the preparation of this product to prevent separation of ingredients. Again, spices, fruits, vegetables, or meats may be added. It may also have a smoked flavor.

COLDPACK CHEESE

known also as Club Cheese is prepared by grinding very fine, and *without* heating, one or more lots of the same cheese or different varieties of cheeses. It is usually made from Cheddar cheese. Other cheeses such as Swiss, Blue, or Limburger are also used. Color and spice may be added and it may have a smoked flavor. The flavor is the same as the cheese used and it usually is aged or sharp. It spreads easily. It is packed in familiar containers, such as jars or crocks, all of which are designed to keep out air.

COLDPACK CHEESE FOOD

is prepared in the same manner as Coldpack Cheese but includes one or more dairy ingredients. The optional dairy ingredients used are cream, milk, skim milk, cheese whey. In addition, sweetening agents such as sugar, dextrose, and corn syrup may be added. Coldpack Cheese Food may contain spices, fruits, vegetables, or meats and may have a smoked flavor. It spreads easily due to the other ingredients added and its higher moisture contents. It is packaged the same as Coldpack Cheese.

CHECKLIST OF CHEESES OF THE WORLD

This checklist is based on the United States Department of Agriculture publication *Cheese Varieties and Descriptions*, 1953 revised 1969.

Alemtejo: Alemtejo is a rather soft cheese. It is made mostly from ewe's milk, but goat's milk is often added, especially for the smaller sizes. Warm milk is curdled, usually with an extract prepared from the flowers of a kind of thistle.

American: American and American-type cheeses are descriptive terms used to identify the group which includes Cheddar (i.e. American Cheddar), Colby, granular or stirred-curd, and washed- or soaked-curd cheeses. Sometimes Monterey or Jack cheese is included in this group. A description of each kind is given under its specific name.

Appenzeller: Appenzeller cheese, which is similar to Swiss, is made from cow's milk in Switzerland. It is made usually from skim milk, but sometimes from whole milk, and soaked in cider or white wine and spices.

Asadero: Asadero is a white, whole-milk Mexican cheese. The curd is heated, and the hot curd is cut and braided or kneaded into loaves of various sizes, ranging from eight ounces to eleven pounds in weight.

Asiago: Asiago cheese originated in the commune of that name in the Province of Vicenza, Italy. It is now made from cow's milk and is a sweet-curd, semi-cooked cheese with a pungent aroma. Like other grating cheeses, it may be used as a table cheese when not aged.

In the United States, three modifications of Asiago are made, namely, fresh (soft), medium and old. The method of manufacture is much the same for all three and is similar to that used for other Italian cheeses, such as fontina, Parmesan, and Romano.

Asin: Asin cheese, which is also called water cheese, is a sour-milk, washed-curd, whitish, soft, buttery, more or less ripened cheese that is made in northern Italy.

Backsteiner: Backsteiner cheese is a modified Limburger-Romadur-type cheese. Backsteiner means brick, and the cheese is so called because of its brick-like shape. However, it is not like the Brick cheese made in the United States but is more like Limburger that is made from partly skimmed milk.

Bagozzo: Bagozzo is a Parmesan-type cheese. It has a hard, yellow body and a rather sharp flavor. The surface often is colored red.

Bakers': Bakers' is a skim-milk cheese that is softer, more homogeneous, and contains more acid than cottage cheese. Bakers' cheese usually is used commercially in making such bakery products as cheese cake, pie, and pastries. Usually it is not offered in retail trade.

Barberey: Barberey is a soft cheese resembling Camembert. It is also commonly known as Fromage de Troyes.

Bellelay: Bellelay, also called monk's head, is a soft, blue-veined, whole-milk cheese that resembles Gorgonzola. It was made originally in the fifteenth century by monks in the Canton of Bern, Switzerland, and now is made exclusively in that locality. It has a soft, buttery consistency and can be spread on bread.

Bel Paese: Bel Paese, which means "beautiful country," is the trade name of one of the best known, most popular of a group of Italian table cheeses. They are uncooked, soft, sweet, mild, and fast-ripened. Similar cheese is marketed in other European countries under other names.

Production of a soft cheese of the Bel Paese type was introduced in the United States in 1938. Because of the Italian trademark, cheese of this type made in the United States is sold under various other names.

Bitto: Bitto is a firm, semicooked cheese of the Swiss group, made in northern Italy. When made from whole milk and not fully cured, it is used as table cheese. When made from skim milk and fully cured, it is grated and used as a condiment.

Bleu: Bleu is the French name for a group of Roquefort-type cheeses made in the Roquefort area in southeastern France from milk other than ewe's milk. It applies also to Roquefort-type cheeses made elsewhere in France. (that is, outside the Roquefort area), regardless of the kind of milk used.

Blue: Blue, blue-mold, or blue-veined cheese is the name for cheese of the Roquefort type that is made in the United States and Canada. It is made from cow's milk, rather than ewe's milk. The French word for this type of cheese is Bleu. Considerable quantities of blue cheese are made in the United States, and cheese of this type is imported from Argentina, Canada, Denmark, France, Finland, and Sweden.

Bondost: Bondost is a Swedish, farm-type, cow's-milk cheese that has been made in Wisconsin for more than thirty years. Sometimes cumin or caraway seed is mixed with the curd just before it is put into the forms.

Bourgain: Bourgain is a type of fresh Neufchatel cheese made in France. However, the fat content is low, the cheese is not salted, it contains a relatively high percentage of moisture, and it is very soft. It is perishable and is consumed locally.

Brick: Brick cheese, one of the few cheeses of American origin, is made in considerable quantities in numerous factories, particularly in Wisconsin. It is a sweet-curd, semisoft, cow's-milk cheese, with a mild but rather pungent and sweet flavor, midway between Cheddar and Limburger but not so sharp as

Cheddar and not so strong as Limburger. The body is softer than Cheddar but firmer than Limburger, is elastic, and slices well without crumbling. Brick has an open texture with numerous round and irregular shaped eyes (holes). Although the exact derivation of the name is unknown, it may refer to its brick-like shape or to the bricks used in pressing.

Brickbat: Brickbat cheese, which was made in Wiltshire, England, as long ago as the eighteenth century, is made from fresh milk to which a small portion of cream is added. The cheese is said to be good to eat for as long as a year after being made.

Brie: Brie, which was first made several centuries ago, is a soft, surface-ripened cheese made usually from cow's whole milk. Brie-type cheese is made also in other parts of France and in other countries, including the United States. Brie is similar to Camembert. Both are ripened partly by molds and bacteria, and probably yeasts, that grow on the surface of the cheese. However, because of differences in the details of manufacture, the internal ripening and characteristic flavor and aroma differ.

Buttermilk: Buttermilk cheese is made from the curd of buttermilk and is somewhat finer grained than cottage cheese, which it closely resembles.

Caciocavallo: Caciocavallo is an Italian plastic-curd (pasta filata) cheese. The cured cheese has a smooth, firm body, and preferably the interior of the cheese is white.

Caciocavallo and provolone are made by almost identical methods. However, Caciocavallo contains less fat than provolone and usually is not smoked, and each is molded in distinctive shapes. Caciocavallo is made usually from cow's milk.

Caciocavallo Sicilano: Caciocavallo Siciliano, a plastic-curd (pasta filata) cheese like the Italian provolone and caciocavallo, is essentially a pressed provolone. It is made chiefly, from cow's whole milk, but sometimes from goat's milk or a mixture of the two.

Cacio Fiore: Cacio Fiore, also called caciotta, is a soft, yellowish, Italian cheese with a delicate, buttery flavor. It is made form ewe's or goat's milk.

Caerphilly: Caerphilly is a semisoft, cow's milk cheese made in Wales. The cheese is white and smooth, lacks elasticity, and is granular rather than waxy when broken.

Camembert: Camembert, a soft, surface-ripened cow's-milk cheese, was first made at Camembert, a hamlet in France. It is said that Napoleon was served this cheese, which was as yet unnamed, and he thereupon named it Camembert. Camembert-type cheese is made also in other parts of France and in other countries, including the United States. The interior is yellow, and waxy, creamy, or almost fluid in consistency, depending on the degree of ripening. The rind is a thin, felt-like layer of gray mold and dry cheese interspersed with patches of reddish yellow. Camembert is made in much the same way as Brie, but it is smaller and the characteristic flavor differs.

Cantal: Cantal, also known locally as Fourme, is a hard, rather yellow cheese with a piquant flavor and firm, close body. It has been made for centuries in the region of the Auvergne Mountains in the Department of Cantal, France.

Caraway: Caraway cheese is a so-called spiced cheese that contains caraway seed.

Carré: Carré or Carré Frais, known also as double créme carré and fromage double créme, is a small, rich French cream cheese of the Neufchatel type. It is made from a rich milk-and-cream mixture. It is eaten fresh. Cheese made in a similar way, with considerable salt added to act as a preservative, is called Demisel.

Carré de l'Est: Carré de l'Est is a Camembert-type cheese made in France from either raw or pasteurized cow's whole milk.

Cheddar: Cheddar cheese is named for the village of Cheddar in Somersetshire, England, where it was first made. The exact date or origin is not known, but it has been made since the latter part of the sixteenth century. Colonial housewives made the first Cheddar cheese in America; and the first cheese factory in the United States was a Cheddar-cheese factory, established in 1851 by Jesse Williams, near Rome, Oneida County, N.Y. It is made and used so widely that it often is called American cheese, or American Cheddar cheese, and cheeses similar to Cheddar but made by a slightly modified process are called American-type cheeses.

Cheddar is a hard cheese, ranging in color from nearly white to yellow. It is made from sweet, whole cow's milk, either raw or pasteurized. (If it is made from partly skimmed or skim milk, it must be so labeled.) Research has shown that pasteurizing the milk improves the quality of the cheese. More than 90 percent of the Cheddar cheese made in the United States is now made from either heat-treated or pasteurized milk.

Cheshire: Cheshire, which also is called Chester, ranks with Cheddar as the oldest and most popular of English cheeses. Cheshire is a firm cheese, but it is more crumbly and not so compact as Cheddar. The curd may be nearly white but more often it is colored deep yellow.

Colby: Colby cheese, which is similar to Cheddar, may be made from either raw or pasteurized milk. It is made in the same way as Cheddar except that the curd is not matted and milled. Colby has a softer body and more open texture than Cheddar cheese, and it contains more moisture.

Cooked: Cooked cheese (German, Kochkäse, literally cook cheese) is so named because it is made by heating or "cooking" cheese curd. It is made not only in the United States but also in many foreign countries. The method of making differs somewhat in different countries and in different localities within a country, and the cheese is known by different local names. In the United States, the local names include cup cheese and Pennsylvania pot cheese. When properly made, cooked cheese has an agreeable flavor and a smooth buttery consistency similar to Camembert. The fresh cheese curd which is the basic ingredient of cooked cheese is made from skim milk, or reconstituted concentrated skim milk or nonfat dry milk solids, or a mixture of any of these.

Coon: Coon cheese is a Cheddar cheese that is cured by a special patented method. The surface of coon cheese is colored very dark; the body is short and crumbly; and the flavor is very sharp and tangy.

Cornhusker: Cornhusker cheese was introduced by the Nebraska Agricultural Experiment Station about 1940. It is similar to Cheddar and colby, but has a softer body, contains more moisture, and takes less time to make. Like brick cheese, cornhusker contains numerous mechanical openings.

Cottage: Cottage cheese, sometimes called pot cheese, is a soft, uncured cheese made from skim milk or from reconstituted concentrated skim milk or non-fat dry milk solids. The large particles of curd resemble kernels of popped corn, and this kind of cheese is called popcorn cheese. Small-grained cottage cheese sometimes is called country-style or farm-style cheese.

Usually some cream is mixed with the cheese curd before it is marketed or consumed. If the cheese contains four percent or more of fat, it is called creamed cottage cheese. Flavoring materials, such as peppers, olives, and pimientos, may be added also.

Coulommiers: Coulommiers cheese, is a soft, mold-ripened, unwashed cheese, made in France. A modified Coulommiers cheese is made in the United States and Canada.

Cream: Cream cheese is a soft, mild, rich, uncured cheese made of cream or a mixture of cream and milk, and used as a spread for bread, in sandwiches, and with salads. It is one of the most popular soft cheeses in the United States. In addition, there are several French cream cheeses.

Crescenza: Crescenza is an uncooked, soft, creamy, mildly sweet, fast-ripening, yellowish cheese of the Bel Paese type. It is made in northern Italy, from cow's whole milk.

Derby: Derby, or Derbyshire, is a hard, sweet-curd cheese made in Derbyshire, England, from cow's whole milk. It is similar to Cheddar but is not so firm and solid, is more flaky when broken, has a higher moisture content, and ripens more rapidly.

Domiati: Domiati, a so-called pickled cheese, is one of the most popular Egyptian cheeses. It is a soft, white cheese with no openings, mild and salty in flavor when fresh and cleanly acid when cured. When it is held for prolonged periods (a year or more) it darkens in color and develops a strong flavor.

Dunlop: Dunlop, a rich, white, pressed cheese made in Scotland, formerly was considered the national cheese of Scotland.

Edam: Edam cheese was first made in the vicinity of Edam in the Province of North Holland, Netherlands. Like Gouda, it is a semisoft to hard, sweet-curd cheese made from cow's milk. Edam is made also in the United States. Edam has a pleasingly mild, clean, sometimes salty, flavor and a rather firm and crumbly body, free of holes and openings.

Egg: Egg cheese, first made in the Province of Nyland, Finland, is made from fresh milk to which fresh eggs are added.

Emiliano: Emiliano is a very hard cheese of the Parmesan type. The flavor varies from mild to rather sharp, and the texture is granular.

Farm: Farm cheese, originally made on farms in France is essentially the same as cottage cheese. In the United States, farm cheese, which is known also as farm-er cheese and pressed cheese, is a firm pressed cheese.

Feta: Feta, a white, so-called pickled cheese, is the principal soft cheese made by the shepherds in the mountainous region near Athens, Greece. It usually is made from ewe's milk but is sometimes made from goat's milk. In the United States it is made from cow's milk.

Flower: Flower cheese is a soft, cured cheese made in England from cow's whole milk. It contains the petals of various kinds of flowers, such as roses or mari-golds, which accounts for its name.

Fontina: Fontina is a cooked-cured, whole-milk, semisoft to hard, slightly yellow cheese with a delicate, nutty flavor and a pleasing aroma. It is made from ewe's milk, and from cow's milk in the United States. When partly cured, it is used as a table cheese; when fully cured, it is hard and is used for grating.

Formaggi di Pasta Filata: Formaggi di Pasta Filata (cheese from plastic curd) refers to a group of Italian cheeses that are made by curdling the milk with rennet, warming and fermenting the curd, heating it until it is plastic, drawing it into ropes and then kneading and shaping it while it is hot and plastic. This unusual manipulation of the curd while it is being drawn and shaped results in cheese that is free of holes and pockets of air and whey and that keeps well even in warm climates. Some plastic-curd cheeses are eaten as table cheese when fresh or after curing only a few months; others are used for grating after long curing which makes them hard and sharp in flavor. Among the best known plastic-cured cheeses are: provolone, Caciocavallo, and mozzarella.

Gammelost: Gammelost, made from sour milk in Norway, is a semisoft, blue-mold, ripened table cheese, with a rather sharp, aromatic flavor.

Gex: Gex, a hard, cow's-milk cheese, is named for the town of Gex in France, where it was first made more than a hundred years ago. It is one of the group of blue-mold cheeses known in France as bleu cheeses.

Gjetost: Gjetost is a Norwegian boiled-whey cheese. The "Gje-" indicates that it is a goat's-milk product. However, it is commonly made from the whey ob-tained when cheese is made from a mixture of cow's milk and not less than ten percent of goat's milk. When cheese is made from goat's milk only and the whey so obtained is made into boiled-whey cheese, it is called ekte (genuine) Gjetost, or Geitmysost.

Gloucester: Gloucester is a hard cheese made in England in the county of Gloucester, for which it is named. Gloucester and Derby are said to be almost identical and are made in practically the same way.

Gorgonzola: Gorgonzola, is the principal blue-green veined cheese of Italy. The interior of the cheese is mottled with blue-green veins like those in Roquefort.

Gouda: Gouda, first made in the vicinity of Gouda in the Province of South Holland, Netherlands, is a semisoft to hard, sweet-curd cheese similar to Edam except that it contains more fat. It is made from whole or partly skimmed cow's milk, but skimmed less than milk used in making Edam.

Gournay: Gournay, is a soft cheese of the fresh Neufchatel type, made in France. It is similar to the cream cheese made in the United States.

Grana: Grana refers to a group of Italian cheeses with the following special characteristics: Granular body and texture (hence the name grana); sharp flavor (they are widely known for intensity and exquisitness of flavor); hardness (they are among the most suitable for grating); very small eyes; good keeping quality, even in hot climates; and excellent shipping properties (they require no careful packaging). There are two main types of grana cheeses: (1) Grana Lombardo, which is made largely in the Province of Larbardy; and (2) Grana Reggiano, which is made largely in Reggio, in the Province of Emilia. Considerable quantities of both types of grana cheeses are exported from Italy, usually under the name Parmesan (the common name outside of Italy, and sometimes in Italy, for these cheeses). Both types are imported into the United States as Parmesan, and Grana Reggiano is also imported as Reggiano Parmesan. Both types are made in the United States and may be known by either name (Parmesan or Reggiano).

Gruyére: Gruyére cheese has been made for more than two hundred years. It is named for the village of Gruyére, in the Canton of Fribourg, Switzerland. Gruyére is made from cow's whole milk in much the same way as Swiss; however, Gruyére is smaller, has smaller eyes and a sharper flavor, and usually is cured in a more humid curing room.

Herrgårdsost: Herrgårdsost (manor cheese) is very popular in Sweden, where it has been made since the 1890's. It has a medium firm, pliable body, a milk, sweet, nutty flavor, and a pleasing aroma. The cured cheese contains eyes similar to those in Gruyére, that is, they are smaller than those in Swiss cheese. Herrgårdsost is made from partly skimmed pasteurized cow's milk.

Incanestrato: Incanestrato (basketed) cheese is so named because the curd often is pressed in wicker molds (baskets). The imprint of the wicker remains on the cheese. As made in Sicily, it is a plastic-curd (pasta filata) cheese made from ewe's milk or a mixture of ewe's milk and cow's milk. Various spices may be added. Pepper may be added, and then it is called pepato. In the United States, incanestrato and also pepato are made from cow's milk, usually by the Romano process.

Islgny: Islgny cheese, which is said to be of American origin, is named for a town in France. It is the same shape as Camembert, and is made like Camembert except that the cheese is washed and rubbed occasionally while it is curing to check the growth of molds on the surface. The ripened cheese has a firmer body than Camembert and has a flavor and aroma like mild Limburger.

Italian: Italian cheese refers not only to varieties now made in Italy, but also to those that originated in Italy and that now are made in other countries as well. Parmesan, Romano, and provolone are among the best known, and they are made in considerable quantities in the United States. The plastic-curd (pasta filata) cheeses include the hard provolone and the soft provole or mozzarella. Pecorino, used with the name of a cheese, indicates that it was made from ewe's milk; caprino, that it was made from goat's milk; and vacchino, that it was made from cow's milk.

Kasseri: Kasseri is a hard cheese made in Greece, usually from ewe's milk.

Katschkawalj: Katschawalj is a plastic-curd, caciocavallo-type cheese made from ewe's milk in Serbia, Rumania, Bulgaria, and Macedonia.

Kosher: Kosher cheese is made especially for Jewish consumers, to conform with Jewish dietary custom. Typically, it is made without animal rennet. Sometimes the milk is curdled by natural souring; sometimes a starter is added to the milk. Among the Kosher cheeses are soft cheeses, like cream and cottage cheese; kosher Gouda; and a cheese that is made by the Limburger process but, unlike Limburger, is eaten fresh. Kosher cheese bears a label by which it can be identified.

Krutt: Krutt, or Kirgischerkäse, is made by the nomadic tribes of the middle Asiatic Steppes from the skim milk of cows, goats, ewes, or camels.

Kuminost: Kuminost, also called Kommenost, is a spiced cheese made in the Scandinavian countries from whole or partly skimmed cow's milk. Cumin and caraway seed are mixed with the curd before it is pressed.

Lancashire: Lancashire cheese is named for the county in England where it is made and where much of it is consumed. It is said to be the most popular cheese in some sections of England. It is similar in shape to Cheshire and Cheddar, but white in color, softer, moister, and has a stronger flavor. The fully cured cheese is said to be especially suitable for toasting and for use in making Welsh rarebit.

Lapland: Lapland cheese, which is like a very hard Swiss, is made by the Laplanders from reindeer milk.

Leather: Leather cheese, also known as leder and as holstein dairy cheese, is made in Germany, from cow's skim milk, with 5 to 10 percent of buttermilk added.

Leyden: Leyden, which is also known as Komijne Kaas, is a spiced cheese made in the Netherlands from partly skimmed cow's milk to which color is added. Caraway and cumin seeds, and sometimes cloves, are added to a portion of the curd.

Liederkranz: Liederkranz is the trade name of a soft, surface-ripened cheese that is made in Ohio from cow's whole milk. It is similar to a very mild Limburger in body, flavor, aroma, and type of ripening.

Limburger: Limburger is a semisoft, surface-ripened cheese with a characteristic strong flavor and aroma. Usually it contains small irregular openings. Limburger was first made in the Province of Lüttich, Belgium, and is named for the town of Limburg, where originally much of it was marketed. It is made also in other parts of Europe, especially in Germany and Austria, and in the United States, especially in Wisconsin and New York.

Liptauer: Liptauer is a soft, so-called pickled cheese that is named for the Province of Liptow in northern Hungary, where it is made. Cheese of this type, either identical or very similar, is made in numerous villages in the Carpathian mountain region of Czechoslovakia and Hungary.

Livarot: Livarot, which is a soft, cow's milk cheese, is named for the village of Livarot, France, where the industry is centralized. Livarot is very much like Camembert.

Loaf: Loaf cheese refers to the rectangular, loaf-like shape in which several cheeses are packaged and marketed, rather than to a specific variety.

Lodigiano: Lodigiano, a Parmesan-type cheese, is made in the vicinity of Lodi, Italy, from which it derives its name. It is larger, contains less fat, has larger eyes, and ripens more slowly than Reggiano. It may be cured for as long as three to four years, and it is used for grating.

Lombardo: Lombardo, a Parmesan-type cheese, is similar to Lodigiano. The cheese has a sharp and aromatic flavor and granular texture.

Lorraine: Lorraine, a small, sour-milk, hard cheese, is named for Lorraine, Germany, where it is made and where it is regarded as a delicacy. It is seasoned with pepper, salt, and pistachio nuts and is eaten while comparatively fresh.

Lüneberg: Lüneberg cheese is made in the small valleys in western Austria. When ripe, the cheese is said to be about midway in characteristics between Swiss and Limburger.

Manteca: Manteca or Manteche "cheese," which is made in Italy, is in reality butter enclosed in a bag of plastic cheese curd. The plastic-curd bag preserves the butter by protecting it from the air, thus preventing its deterioration even in a warm climate.

Mont d'Or: Mont d'Or, a soft cheese similar to Pont l'Évêque, is named for Mont d'Or, near Lyon, in the Department of Rhône, France, where it is said to have been made for more than three hundred years. It formerly was made from goat's milk, but now usually is made from cow's milk to which a small quantity of goat's milk may be added.

Monterey: Monterey (or Jack) cheese was first made on farms in Monterey County, California, about 1892, and manufacture on a factory scale began about 1916. The name Monterey has largely replaced Jack, except for the type known as high-moisture Jack.

The cheese is made from pasteurized whole, partly skimmed, or skim milk. Whole-milk Monterey is semisoft; Monterey made from partly skimmed or skim milk (called grating-type Monterey, dry Monterey, or dry Jack) is hard and is used for grating. High-moisture Jack is made from whole milk by a slightly different process.

Mozzarella: Mozzarella is a soft, plastic-curd cheese that is made in some parts of Latium and Campania in southern Italy. It originally was made only from buffalo's milk, but now it is made also from cow's milk. It is used for the most part in cooking. Considerable Mozzarella is made in the United States.

Münster: Münster is a semisoft, whole-milk cheese.

Mysost: Mysost cheese is made in the Scandinavian countries and in the United States, from the whey obtained in the manufacture of other cheeses. It is light brown in color, has a buttery consistency and a mild, sweetish flavor.

Natural Rindless Loaf: Natural Rindless Loaf cheese is natural cheese that is packaged and marketed in a transparent, flexible wrapper by one of several variations of a method that was developed about 1940. Large quantities of various kinds of cheese, including brick, Cheddar, and Swiss, are now marketed in this way.

Neufchâtel: Neufchâtel cheese, as made originally in France, is a soft, mild cheese made from whole or skim milk or a mixture of milk and cream. It may be eaten fresh or it may be cured. In the United States, Neufchâtel is made from pasteurized milk or a pasteurized milk-and-cream mixture in much the same way as cream cheese but it contains less fat and more moisture.

Noekkelost: Noekkelost (or Nögelost), which is a Norwegian spiced cheese, is similar to other spiced cheeses such as Kuminost and Dutch Leyden. Cumin seed, cloves, and sometimes caraway seed are the spices used. In Norway, Noekkelost usually is made from partly skimmed milk; in the United States, it may be made from either whole or partly skimmed milk.

Olivet: Olivet is a soft, cow's-milk cheese, made in France. There are three types of Olivet: (1) Unripened, made from whole milk, sometimes with cream added. This is consumed as fresh, summer, white, or cream cheese. (2) Half-ripened or blue, made from whole or partly skimmed milk. This is the most common type. (3) Ripened, also made from whole or partly skimmed milk.

Parmesan: Parmesan is the name in common use outside of Italy, and sometimes in Italy, for a group of very hard cheeses that have been made and known in that country for centuries as grana. Included in the group are Parmigiano, Reggiano, Lodigiano, Lombardy, Emiliano, Veneto or Venezza, and Bagozzo or Bresciano. They differ in size and shape and in the extent to which the milk is skimmed, and there are slight differences in the methods of manufacture. Fully cured Parmesan is very hard but keeps almost indefinitely. It can be grated easily, and is used as grated cheese on salads and soups, and with macaroni. Considerable quantities are imported into the United States for use as grated cheese.

Parmigiano: Parmigiano, which is about the same as Reggiano, is one of the subvarieties of grana (commonly called Parmesan), the hard Italian cheeses used for grating.

Pasta Filata: Pasta Filata (plastic curd) are Italian cheeses characterized by the fact that, after the whey is drained off, the curd is immersed in hot water or hot whey and is worked, stretched, and molded while it is in a plastic condition. The principal varieties of pasta filata cheeses are: Hard cheeses—Caciocavallo, provolone, and provolette; soft, moist cheeses—mozzarella, provole, Scamorze, and provatura.

Pickled: Pickled cheese is the term used to describe a group of cheeses to which considerable salt is added in order to prolong their keeping quality. They usually are soft cheeses with a white curd and are made in warm climates, principally in the countries bordering on the Mediterranean Sea. The salt may be added either to the milk or to the curd, or the cheese may be packed in either salt brine or dry salt.

Pimento: Pimento cheese is any cheese to which ground pimientos have been added.

Pont l'Évêque: Pont l'Évêque, a soft cheese similar to Romadur, is manufactured in France. It is mold-ripened like Camembert, but has a firmer body and is a yellower color.

Port du Salut: Port du Salut (or Port Salut) cheese was first made about 1865 by Trappist Monks at the abbey at Port du Salut, France. Its manufacture has spread to abbeys in various parts of Europe, especially Austria, Czechoslovakia, and southern Germany, and also to Canada and to the United States, where it is made in at least one monastery in Kentucky.

The curd of Port du Salut cheese is compact and elastic, similar to Pont l'Évêque; the flavor is similar to Gouda; and in some instances the aroma is like very mild Limburger.

Process: Process (or pasteurized Process) cheese is made by grinding fine, and mixing together by heating and stirring, one or more cheeses of the same, or two or more varieties. An emulsifying agent is then added to the mixture and the whole worked into a homogeneous, plastic mass. Lactic, citric, acetic, or phosphoric acid or vinegar, a small amount of cream, water, salt, color, and spices or flavoring materials may be added. The cheese may be smoked, or it may be made from smoked cheese, or so-called liquid smoke or smoke "flavor" may be added.

Provolone: Provolone, an Italian plastic-curd (pasta filata) cheese, was first made in southern Italy but is now also made in other parts of Italy and in the United States. It is light in color, mellow, smooth, cuts without crumbling, and has an agreeable flavor.

Queso Blanco: Queso Blanco is the principal Latin-American cheese. The cheese is made from whole, partly skimmed, or skim milk; or from whole milk with cream or skim milk added.

Ricotta: Ricotta cheese is made from the coagulable material (principally albumin) in the whey obtained in the manufacture of other cheese, such as Cheddar, Swiss, and provolone.

Romadur: Romadur is a soft, ripened cheese made in southern Germany, especially in Bavaria, from either whole or partly skimmed cow's milk. It is similar to Limburger and has the same origin, but is smaller, has a milder aroma, and contains less salt.

Romano: Romano, which is sometimes called incanestrato, is one of the most popular of the very hard Italian cheeses. It is used as a table cheese after curing for five to eight months, and after longer curing—usually at least a year—it is hard, very sharply piquant, and suitable for grating.

Roquefort: Roquefort, a blue-veined, semisoft to hard cheese, is named for the village of Roquefort in the Department of Aveyron in southeastern France, where its manufacture has been an important industry for more than two centuries. A French regulation limits use of the word Roquefort to cheese made in the Roquefort area from ewe's milk. Other French cheese of the Roquefort type is called bleu cheese, and Roquefort-type cheese made in the United States and other countries is known as blue cheese.

Roquefort cheese is characterized by its sharp, peppery, piquant flavor, and the mottled, blue-green veins throughout the curd and the whiteness of the curd between the veins. Powder containing spores of *Penicillium roqueforti* mold is added to the curd as it is being put into the hoops, and the veins result from growth of the mold during the curing period. The powder is prepared by inocculating loaves of fresh bread with a pure culture of mold; when the mold has permeated the bread—in four to six weeks—the interior is crumbled, dried, ground, sifted, and stored for use in the cheese.

Runesten: Runesten cheese, which was first made in Denmark, is made also in the United States. The cured cheese resembles Swiss cheese, but the eyes are smaller and each "wheel" is much smaller.

Saanen: Saanen, is a hard cheese similar to Swiss. It is made from cow's milk in Switzerland, where its manufacture dates back to the sixteenth century. The curd is very firm, and in aged cheese it is brittle and deep yellow in color. It is not unusual for a cheese to be accorded great honor in a household and for it to be kept for many decades. It is the custom to make a cheese at the birth of a child and to eat portions of the cheese on feast days during his life and at his burial and also to honor his descendents on similar occasions. It is said that one cheese was kept for such use for two hundred years.

Sage: Sage cheese is an American-type, spiced (sage flavored) cheese made by either the Cheddar or granular or stirred-curd process.

Sapsago: Sapsago cheese has been made in the Canton of Glarus, Switzerland, for at least five hundred years and perhaps more. It is a small, very hard cheese that frequently is dried. A powder prepared from clover leaves is added to the curd, which gives it a sharp, pungent flavor, a pleasing aroma, and a light-green or sage-green color.

Schloss: Schloss cheese is a small, soft, ripened cheese made in Germany and northern Austria. It is very much like Romadur, that is, similar to but milder than Limburger.

Serra da Estrella: Serra da Estrella, which is named for the Serra da Estrella mountain range along which it is made, is the most highly prized of several kinds of cheese made in Portugal. It is rather soft and has a pleasing, acid flavor.

Spiced: Spiced cheese is cheese to which one or more spices are added during the making process in such a way that the spices are distributed evenly throughout the finished cheese. Spices used include caraway seed, cumin or cumin seed, pepper, cloves, anise, and sage.

Stilton: Stilton, considered by many people to be the finest English cheese, is a hard, mild, blue-veined, cow's-milk cheese. High-quality cheese of this type is also made in the United States.

Stilton, which is one of the mold-ripened group of blue-veined cheeses that includes French Roquefort and Italian Gorgonzola, is rich and mellow and has a piquant flavor; however, it is milder than either Roquefort or Gorgonzola.

Surati: Surati (or Panir) cheese, which is made from buffalo's milk, is perhaps the best known of the few varieties of cheese made in India. The cheese is uncolored and is characterized by the fact that it is kept in whey while it cures and is transported in whey in large earthen containers. It is supposed to have therapeutic properties.

Sweet-curd: Sweet-curd cheese in the United States refers to cheese made by the usual Cheddar process, except that the milk is not ripened and the curd is cut, heated, and drained rather quickly, without waiting for the development of acidity, and the curd is not milled. In other respects, the process is similar to the Cheddar process, and the cured cheese is much like Cheddar cheese but usually contains more moisture and the curd is not so compact. Such varieties as brick, Münster, Edam, and Gouda are also sweet-curd cheeses.

Swiss: Swiss (Emmentaler) cheese, which is a large, hard, pressed-curd cheese with an elastic body and a mild, nut-like, sweetish flavor, is best known because of the holes or eyes that develop in the curd as the cheese ripens. The eyes often are one-half to one inch in diameter and from one to three inches apart. Switzerland is famous for this so-called King of Cheeses, and a large part of the milk produced in Switzerland is used in its production. It was first made, probably about the middle of the fifteenth century, in the Canton of Bern in the Emmental Valley (which accounts for its native name Emmentaler).

Tilsiter: Tilsiter is a cow's-milk cheese that was first made by immigrants from the Netherlands who settled in the vicinity of Tilsit in East Prussia. It is a medium-firm, slightly yellow, plastic cheese, similar to brick cheese. It has a mild to medium-sharp piquant flavor, similar to mild Limburger. Sometimes caraway seed is added to skim-milk Tilsiter.

Trappist: Trappist cheese was first made in 1885 in a monastery in Yugoslavia. It is made also in monasteries in Hungary, Czechoslovakia, southern Germany, and other parts of Europe. The cheese is pale yellow and has a mild flavor. Although it is a semisoft cheese, it is cured more like the hard cheeses. Trappist cheese is made from fresh, whole milk, usually cow's milk but some ewe's or goat's milk may be added.

Travnik: Travnik, is a soft cheese made from ewe's milk to which a small proportion of goat's milk is added. Usually it is made from whole milk, but sometimes skim milk is used. The fresh, whole-milk cheese is soft, almost white, and mild and pleasing in flavor.

Washed-curd: Washed-curd (or soaked-curd) cheese is a semisoft to slightly firm cheese that is made in the same way as Cheddar except that the milled curd is washed with water before it is salted. "Soaked curd" usually indicated a longer washing period than "washed curd." Washing the curd increases the moisture content of the cheese, reduces the lactose content and final acidity, decreases body firmness, and increases openness of texture. Washed-curd cheese does not keep as well as Cheddar.

Weisslacker: Weisslacker, so named because of its white, smeary, lustrous, surface, is a soft, ripened, cow's-milk cheese similar to Limburger and backsteiner that is made in Bavaria. In some localities it is well ripened and has a strong flavor and is called bierkase.

Wensleydäle: Wensleydäle, named for the District of Wensleydäle in Yorkshire, England, where it was first made, is a medium hard, blue-veined cheese made from cow's whole milk.

Zomma: Zomma, made in Turkey, is a plastic-curd, Caciocavallo-type cheese that is very much like Katschkawalj.

NOW THAT YOU ASK...

Q. What country is the biggest producer of cheese?

A. The United States is the world's biggest producer. It manufactured close to one million *tons* in 1970.

Q. What, exactly, is cheese?

A. The Food and Drug Administration defines cheese as "a product made from curd obtained from the whole, partly skimmed, or skimmed milk of cows, or from milk of other animals, with or without added cream, by coagulating with rennet, lactic acid, or other suitable enzyme or acid, and with or without further treatment of the separated curd by heat or pressure, or by means of ripening ferments, special molds, or seasoning."

Q. What is rennet or lactic acid?

A. They are "starters" used to bring about the separation of milk into curds and whey.

Q. What's the difference between a processed cheese and a natural cheese?

A. A *natural* cheese is the product as it is originally made. A *processed* cheese is a blend of two or more varieties of natural cheeses by heating to yield a constantly uniform flavor and texture. There are variations of processed cheeses such as "cheese food" and "cheese spread." For a full explanation see pages 54 and 63.

Q. What is meant by a "hand" cheese?

A. Originally this cheese was molded to its final shape by hand, thus its name. It has a very strong aroma.

Q. Does mold on cheese mean that it's spoiled?

A. It's not harmful. If there is a surface mold, cut off the molded area. The remaining cheese is still good. Air-tight containers or packaging will lessen the chance of mold occuring.

Q. What makes blue cheese blue?

A. The blue is a mold that is purposely introduced into the cheese to give it its characteristic piquant flavor. The blue penicillium molds (*Penicillium roqueforti*) are mixed with the curd and the cheese is allowed to ripen in high humidity while the molds grow throughout the cheese. There are over fifty varieties of blue cheese with the most famous being Roquefort (France), Stilton (England), Gorgonzola (Italy), and Danablu (Denmark).

Q. Why does Swiss cheese have holes?

A. The holes in Swiss cheese are the result of carbon dioxide bubbles throughout the cheese. The bubbles are caused by propionic acid (*Propionibacterium shermanii*) that has been introduced into the cheese. The acid also gives Swiss cheese its mellow nut-like flavor.

Q. What gives some cheeses their distinct odor?

A. The so called "strong cheeses" are bacteria ripened soft cheeses. The bacteria (*Brevibacterium linens*) works on both the milk and butterfat to produce a rancid bouquet. The strength of the cheese is determined by the amount of surface area exposed to the bacteria.

Q. What is the nutritive value of cheese?

A. Cheese is one of the most concentrated of foods. A pound of cheese may contain the protein and fat of approximately a gallon of milk. It ranks high as a protein source and as a source of calcium and phosphorous. For example, one and one-fourth ounces of Cheddar cheese has about the same amount of protein and calcium as a cup of milk.

Q. What is the calorie content of cheese?

A. Cheeses differ. The chart gives a comparison of a few cheeses:

American	1 medium slice	110 calories
Blue	1 ounce	105 calories
Cheddar type cheese food	1 ounce	90 calories
Cream cheese	1 ounce	105 calories
Creamed cottage cheese	1 ounce	30 calories
Process Cheddar cheese	1 ounce	105 calories
Swiss	1 medium slice	105 calories
Uncreamed cottage cheese	1 ounce	25 calories

Q. How digestable is cheese?

A. Experiments have shown cheese to be highly digestible. From 81 to 97 percent of cheese is fully absorbed by the body.

Q. What kind of milk is used to make cheese?
A. Cheeses have been made from almost all the milks available such as cow (raw, pasteurized, whole, skimmed), Sheep, goat, buffalo, camel, reindeer, and even yak.

Q. Can cheese be made at home?
A. Yes. Almost all the cheese of the world started out as a "home industry." Some types are more difficult than others to make with the easiest being the un- ripened cheeses. For methods of making cheese at home see page 82.

Q. Do I need special equipment to make cheese?
A. Most of the equipment is fairly standard but you will need a "starter." See page 84.

Q. How should cheese be stored?
A. Cheese should be stored to keep out the air but to retain its moisture. Alumi- num foil, plastic wrap, covered containers, or a brine or milk solution, will act to seal off the air. If a cheese is refrigerated when purchased it should be kept refrig- erated. Process cheese, cheese food, or cheese spreads may be stored at room temperature until opened. Once opened, store in the refrigerator.

To make a brine solution, combine:
½ teaspoon salt
½ cup water
 1 tablespoon dry wine or lemon juice
Soak a clean cloth in the solution; then wring out thoroughly. Wrap cheese tightly in the cloth; then wrap in a plastic bag or aluminum foil. (If mold does form, cut it off.) Keep cheese in a cool, dry place.

To make a milk solution boil enough milk to cover the cheese that has been placed in a container. Cool milk and pour over the cheese. Refrigerate.

Q. Can cheese be frozen?
A. Most cheeses become crumbly and flaky when frozen. However, small quan- tities (one pound or less; one inch thick or less) of the following cheeses may be frozen satisfactory: Cheddar, Swiss, Edam, Gouda, Muenster, brick, Port du Salut, provolone, mozzarella, Camembert, and cream. Also, the blue-veined cheeses may be frozen to use for salads or salad dressings where a crumbly texture is desired. They should not be frozen for more than six months.

Q. Is there another way of saying cheese?
A. Yes:

Danish - ost	Polish - ser
Dutch - kaas	Portuguese - queijo
French - fromage	Rumanian - brînză
German - käse	Russian - syr
Greek - terí	Spanish - queso
Hungarian - sajt	Swedish - ost
Italian - fromage	Serbo-Croatian - sir
Irish - cāise	Swahili - jibini
Lithuanian - sūris or kieža	Welsh - caws

Q. What is considered the world's richest cheese?
A. Triple-cream cheese from France is considered to be the ultimate in a rich cheese. Cream is added to an already rich cheese until 100 grams contain 75 percent butterfat. It has the consistency of an eclair.

Q. Did the astronauts bring back any evidence that the moon is made of cheese?
A. In a report in *Science* magazine, June 26, 1970, physicists who tested the moon rocks brought back by Apollo XI found that the lunar rock samples had a compressional velocity very close to that of Muenster, Swiss, and Vermont Cheddar cheese.

THE COOKING WAYS OF CHEESE...

Grate, dice, or cube cheese just before combining with other ingredients.

Melt cheese in top part of double boiler over simmering heat.

Stir grated cheese into completely cooked white sauce; then heat only to melt the cheese.

Process cheese melts and blends easily, but a little extra is needed in a recipe because of its milder flavor.

Sharp, longer-aged natural cheeses add more flavor to cooked dishes than a milder, less-ripened one.

Bake cheese casseroles at low to moderate temperatures.

Add a cheese topping only minutes before removing baking dish from oven.

If a cheese dish is cooked over the stove burner, set on low and stir constantly.

One-half pound of cheese yields about two cups of grated cheese.

Whip cream cheese and use as a topping for deep-dish pies, fruit compotes, or cobblers.

CHEESE-SPICE CHART

Add ¼ teaspoon of:
Ground allspice to cottage cheese dressings
Crushed basil to cream cheese for stuffed celery
Crushed caraway seed to mild cheese spreads
Dill seed to cottage cheese appetizers
Fresh crushed mint to cottage cheese salads
Crushed oregano to sharp cheese spreads
Fresh crushed parsley flakes to cheese balls
Crushed rosemary to cheese sauces
Crushed sage to cheese spreads

MAKE YOUR OWN COTTAGE CHEESE

While there is a steadily rising popularity in making bread at home, it's rare to find someone who makes his own cheese to go with that homemade bread.

Cheese is not as simple to make as yogurt, but it can be an interesting home project. The easiest cheese to make is cottage cheese, which is an unripened cheese and needs no pressing or long-time care.

The basic concern in cheese making is to coagulate the milk and separate it into curds (soft) and whey (liquid). In these recipes, fresh cultured buttermilk is used as a "starter" for this purpose. In order to speed-up the curdling and shorten the cheese-making process, rennet tablets are also used. Rennet tablets can usually be purchased in groceries or drugstores.

Two recipes for making cottage cheese are given. One recipe is a simple one which is a good introduction for making cheese. The other recipe is a more thorough one and is a basis for making other cheeses.

You will need the following equipment:

A double boiler that will hold a ½ gallon of milk. The water in the bottom pan should come around the sides to the same level as the milk in the inner container. (Do not use galvanized metal or aluminum containers.)

A metal spatula or knife long enough to reach the bottom of the pan.

A thermometer capable of measuring 75° to 110°F.

A measuring cup.

A colander and cheesecloth.

SIMPLE COTTAGE CHEESE RECIPE

One gallon of skim milk makes about one pound of cheese. But since this is probably your first attempt at making cheese, let's start with a half gallon of milk.

½ **gallon** *skim* **milk**   ¼ **of a rennet tablet**
½ **cup fresh cultured buttermilk**   1 **teaspoon salt**
   (the starter)

Preparing the Milk:
Warm the milk in a double boiler to 86°F. adding ½ cup buttermilk while it heats. Let stand 45 minutes, keeping a constant temperature between 86° and 88°F. Dissolve the ¼ rennet tablet in 2 tablespoons cold water. Stir thoroughly into milk. Remove milk from heat. Let stand at room temperature until it thickens and curd is formed in about 3 to 6 hours. *DO NOT STIR*. (Curd will be firm like jello, but not hard or brittle) Make sure temperature remains constant. Curd should peel away easily from sides when it is done.

Cutting the Curd:
Using a spatula or knife, cut curd into bits about ½ to 1-inch square all the way to bottom of container. (The liquid whey will rise to the top after a few minutes.)

Cooking the Curd:
After the whey has risen, gently stir pieces to keep them separated. Slowly raise the temperature to 100°F. This should take about 20 minutes, stirring occasionally. Curd particles will resemble cottage cheese. Hold temperature there 10 to 30 minutes. The longer it is heated the drier the cheese will be.

Draining the Curd:
Drain off some of the whey liquid and pour ice water over the curd. Stir and drain this off. Repeat 2 or 3 times, draining water each time.

Salting the Curd:
Pour enough liquid off, from the last cold water application, until just enough liquid remains to completely cover the curds. Add 1 teaspoon of salt and stir gently. Strain off all remaining liquid and true cheese will remain. Let cheese stand in strainer covered with a cheesecloth to allow excess whey to thoroughly drain off. Refrigerate.

Creaming the Curd (*optional*):
To make creamed cottage cheese, add 4 to 6 tablespoons of sweet or sour cream or half and half for each pound of curd. Mix thoroughly.

FUNDAMENTAL COTTAGE CHEESE

This second method of making cottage cheese is more elaborate but it is a very fundamental recipe. Once you master this method, you can go on to making hard cheese since the early steps are necessarily the same for both.

As discussed in the Simple Cottage Cheese Recipe, a starter is needed to begin the cheese-forming process. The starter used in this recipe is fresh cultured buttermilk.

Cottage cheese made without rennet is small-curd and high acid. The cheese made with rennet is the more popular large-curd, low acid type. The method that follows is made with rennet.

You will need the following equipment:

1 gallon container — stainless steel, enamelware or heavily tinned. Do not use galvanized metal or aluminum container.

A container somewhat larger than the 1 gallon container. It will be used to heat water as the bottom part of a double boiler.

Thermometer capable of measuring temperature 75° to 175°F.
Measuring cup
Knife with a blade long enough to reach the bottom of gallon container
Cheesecloth about 18-inches square, fine mesh
Colander
Mixing bowl made of anything but aluminum or galvanized metal
Long spoon or whisk

FUNDAMENTAL COTTAGE CHEESE RECIPE

½ tablespoon buttermilk   **1 gallon pasteurized skim milk**
1 pint pasteurized skim milk   **¼ rennet tablet**
(½ cup fresh cultured buttermilk   **2 tablespoons cool water**
may be used instead of the above)

Preparing Starter:
Combine buttermilk with ½ pint skim milk. Keep this inoculated skim milk at
room temperature, 70° to 75°F. for 16 to 24 hours or until it curdles. Using a
sterilized teaspoon, add a ½ teaspoon of the curdled milk to a ½ pint of fresh
pasteurized skim milk. Let this second culture also curdle, about 12 to 18 hours.
This is your starter and is now ready to use. (You may simply use ½ cup of fresh
cultured buttermilk for your starter-culture.)

Preparing Rennet:
Dissolve ¼ rennet tablet in 2 tablespoons cool water.

Preparing the Milk:
Half fill the larger container with water; then place the gallon containing the milk
inside the other container to form a double boiler arrangement. Heat the water to
bring the milk to room temperature, about 72°F. The milk should be kept at this
room temperature throughout the cheesemaking process until the final stage.
While the milk is heating add ½ cup of your starter-culture (or you may substi-
tute ½ cup of fresh cultured buttermilk for your starter-culture). Let mixture
stand 30 minutes. Add the rennet solution; stir milk thoroughly for 1 minute.

Curdling the Milk:
Allow the milk to stand in the double boiler at room temperature (between
72°-80°F) for 12 to 18 hours. *Do not stir.* To test the curd's firmness, insert a
knife or a spatula along the rim of the inside of the container and gently pull the
curd toward the center. If the curd breaks quickly and smoothly, it is ready to be
cut.

Cutting the Curd:
With a long knife, cut the curds all the way to the bottom in ½-inch squares, up and down columns. Then holding the knife at a slight angle cut down *through* the curd columns to make ½-inch curds underneath, all the way to the bottom; then turn the pail and again make the same angular cuts.

Heating the Cut Curd:
Carefully add water to the outer container to raise its level about ¼-inch above the level of curd and whey in the inner container. Heat the water slowly to raise the temperature of the curd and whey to 110°F. in 30 to 40 minutes. This means a temperature increase of about 1° per minute. While heating, stir every 4 or 5 minutes. The curd should firm up at this temperature. If it doesn't, heat to 115° or 120°F. When curd and whey reach 110°F., heat faster and stir more frequently so that the temperature reaches 115° in 10 to 15 minutes. Hold at this temperature 20 to 30 minutes or until the pieces are firm and do not break easily when squeezed. (If necessary heat to 120° or even to 125°F.) *Stir constantly.* When the curd is firm enough, remove from heat.

Removing the Whey (or getting the whey out of the way):
When the curd is sufficiently firmed, remove most of the whey with a measuring cup. Set colander into a sink or into a pan; spread cheesecloth over it. Pour the remaining curd and whey onto the cheesecloth. Allow curd to drain 2 or 3 minutes, but not much longer or the curd-particles might stick together.

Washing and Cooling Curd:
Bring corners of cheesecloth together. Immerse both cloth and curd in a pan of cool water. Rinse by lowering the cheesecloth several times into the water. Rinse 3 to 5 minutes longer using ice-water to chill the curd. Replace cheesecloth in colander until whey drains completely.

Salting the Curd:
Place curd in a mixing bowl. Add a teaspoon of salt for each pound of curd. Mix thoroughly.

Creaming the Curd (optional):
To make creamed cottage cheese, add 4 to 6 tablespoons of sweet or sour cream or half and half for each pound of curd. Mix thoroughly.

Congratulations on your finished cheese. Place it in a covered container and refrigerate.

If congratulations are not in order and your cheese did not turn out, the following checklist might help:

If the curds are tough and dry:
  You cut the curd into finer strips than necessary
  The curd was held at too high a temperature
  The curd was held too long between cooking and dipping the whey in water
If the curds are soft and wet:
  The curd was allowed to form into larger particles
  The curd was heated at too high or too low a temperature
If there is an off taste or yeasty flavor:
  Unclean utensils may have been used
  An impure starter was used
If there is a sour acid taste:
  Not enough whey was removed from the curd
  The curd was not washed and drained well

BASIC HARD CHEESE

Equipment:
You will need the same equipment as used in the Fundamental Cottage Cheese recipe. But you will also need an extra piece of cheesecloth folded over double, 3 inches wide, rounded into a circle about 5 inches across and pinned in place.

Press:
You will need a press. A simple dead-weight press is adequate.
  Take 2 one-inch thick boards approximately 10" x 12" and drill 2 holes in each board 8-inches apart to fit 1" dowels, as illustrated below.
  You will also need four bricks to place on the top board as weights.

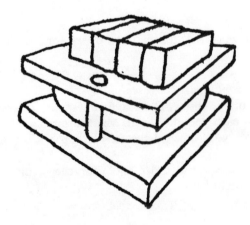

HARD CHEESE RECIPE

1 gallon whole milk
1 cup fresh cultured buttermilk
Cheese color tablet or liquid
  (optional) Follow manufacturer's
  directions.

¼ rennet tablet
2 tablespoons salt
You will also need 1 paraffin block

Combine milk and buttermilk, cover with a clean cloth or plastic wrap, and let stand at room temperature (72°F.) for 6 to 12 hours until curdling develops. Heat the milk over low heat in double boiler to 86°F. (If a yellow cheese is desired, stir the color tablet or liquid into the milk. Dilute according to manufacturer's directions) Dissolve ¼ rennet tablet in 2 tablespoons cold water and add to milk, stirring thoroughly for one minute. (Do not put color and rennet in the milk at the same time.) Let milk stand *without stirring* until curd forms. To test the curd's firmness, insert a knife or a spatula along the inside of the container and gently pull the curd toward the center. If the curd breaks quickly and smoothly, it is ready to be cut.

Cutting the Curd:
With a long knife, cut the curds all the way to the bottom in ½-inch square, up and down columns. Then holding the knife at a slight angle cut down *through* the curd columns to make ½-inch curds underneath, all the way to the bottom; then turn the pail and again make the same angular cuts.

Heating the Cut Curd:
Stir the curds carefully with a long spoon or whisk for about 15 minutes; then heat slowly to 102°F. raising the temperature 1° every 5 minutes. Stir frequently. At the end of heating, curd should hold its shape but collapse after being held in your hand for a few minutes. Remove from heat. Let stand for 1 hour, stirring every 5 minutes.

Removing the Whey:
Set colander into a sink or into a pan; spread cheesecloth over it. Pour the curd and whey onto the cheesecloth. Allow curd to drain 2 or 3 minutes. Sprinkle 1 tablespoon salt over curd, mix with spoon or with whisk; then add another table-spoon salt and mix again. Tie the ends of the cheesecloth together at the top and hang cheese sack for ½ to ¾ hour to drain.

Pressing the Curd:
Pour cheese curd into circular cheese cloth and press down to smooth and level the top. Place 3 or 4 pieces of cheesecloth on top and bottom of the curds and put the cheese on the lower board of the press. Press down on the top board and put 2

bricks on top. About 6 hours later turn the cheese over and put 4 bricks on top. Let stand overnight. Remove all the cloths from the cheese and let stay on the board without the bricks on top for 6 hours, turning frequently until rind is entirely dry.

Storing the Cheese:
Heat paraffin to 210-220°F. Dip the cheese into the paraffin ½ side at a time, holding it there for 1 minute. Store cheese in a cool place. Turn each day for 3 days then 3 times each week. Cheese is mature and ready to eat after 3 to 4 weeks.

MAKING EMMENTHAL CHEESE AT HOME

The following recipe for making a one pound Emmenthal cheese is based on a chart from the Switzerland Cheese Association of New York City. It is used with their permission.

A press is not needed in this recipe as the weight of the curds is sufficient to remove the excess whey.

You will need the following equipment:
Thermometer
8-inch long whisk
Knife with blade about 8-inches long
6 quart pot
Hoop (take an empty gallon-size can and pierce about 60 holes with an awl from the inside to outside)
Ladle
Wooden grate (made from wooden sticks nailed closely together to two transom pieces or use a fine meshed wire screen)
Two large and deep bowls whose diameter is larger than the hoop.
A 12-inch square of cotton or linen.

EMMENTHAL CHEESE RECIPE

5½ quarts milk   ½ cup water
  1 rennet tablet   1 heaping teaspoon yogurt

Combine yogurt and milk; then mix well. Allow mixture to stand for twenty-five minutes. Remove 1 quart of milk and heat the remaining 4½ quarts to 110°F.

stirring constantly. Continue stirring and add the remaining quart of milk to the heated milk to cool it to 88°-90°F. Add the rennet solution to the milk. Let the milk stand for 20-25 minutes. Do not stir.

Cutting the Curd:
With the knife, cut the curd formation into ½ inch square columns. Let the cut curd rest for four or five minutes. With the whisk, break the columns of curd using a figure-eight motion. Let the curd set for three minutes. Repeat this step two more times. It will take about 15 minutes. The bits of curd should be about the size of corn kernels.

Heating the Cut Curd:
Reheat the curds, stirring constantly, to 88°-90°F. Note: This is a crucial step. Do not heat above 92°F. This step takes about five minutes. Remove the pot from the heat, still stirring constantly for five to ten minutes more.

Removing the Whey:
Place the hoop (the can with the holes) on the wooden or wire grate and then place in the sink. Using the ladle, remove the curd from the pot and place in the hoop. Take care to ensure the form is filled evenly and smooth out the top to make it flat. Let the mold stand at room temperature for twenty-four hours. After the first six hours the cheese is turned. It is firm enough to remove from the mold for turning. It is turned again once or twice during the twenty-four hour period.

Salting the Curd:
The cheese is then taken from the mold and placed on the wooden or wire grate. Salt it with one teaspoon of salt over the upper surface and the sides. When the salt has dissolved, rub it in slightly with your fingertips. Immediately put the cheese in a cool place (58°F.). The following day, turn the cheese and salt the untreated surface and again salt the sides. (Instead of salting the cheese you may use a salt bath method. Add four ounces of salt to a quart of water and soak the cheese in it for three hours, turning once half way through so that both sides are equally treated).

Curing the Cheese:
Cure the cheese at 55°F. To ensure the proper humidity fill one bowl two-thirds full of water. Place the grate with the cheese on top of the bowl and then cover the cheese with the second bowl. Let cheese rest for two to three days. After this resting period, the cheese should be turned once a day for the entire curing period, three to five weeks. Each time you turn the cheese, wash and dry the grate. The top surface of the cheese should be lightly cleaned with a cloth dampened with salt water (2 teaspoons salt in ½ quart water— enough to last the

duration of the curing period) and massaged gently to spread moisture evenly. *Do not rub or wash.* A white, then a pinkish hue will develop on the rind. Depending on the temperature used in curing, the cheese is finished in three to five weeks.

APPETIZERS

Cheese served on whole wheat wafers or on thin slices of pumpernickel bread gives the hostess the opportunity to acquaint her guests with the wide world of domestic and foreign cheeses. Serve hard and soft cheeses to satisfy various preferences or combine a mild cheese, such as Muenster or Port du Salut, with a strong cheese, such as Limburger.

Everyone should enjoy and savor a cheese appetizer.

AEGEAN APPETIZERS

½ **cup butter**
¼ **cup grated kefaloteri cheese**

Cream butter. Mix in cheese. Spread on wheat crackers.
Yield: about ¾ cup.

⅓ **cup butter**
¼ **pound kasseri cheese**
Lemon juice

Melt butter over very low heat. Cut cheese into 1-inch cubes. Fry in butter until golden. Place on serving dish and sprinkle with lemon juice.
Yield: 4 to 6 servings.

½ **pound feta cheese**   1 **green pepper, finely chopped**
½ **cup butter, softened**   1 **small onion, finely chopped**
12 **black Greek olives, pitted,**
   chopped

Cut cheese into small pieces; then blend with butter until consistency of whipped cream. Place in serving bowl. Mix in olives, green pepper, and onions. Chill until firm.

Celery stalks
½ cup crumbled feta cheese

1 tablespoon mayonnaise
1 teaspoon Worcestershire sauce

Clean and cut celery stalks in 1½-inch slices. Combine cheese, mayonnaise, and Worcestershire sauce. Mix well. Stuff celery with cheese mixture. Chill.

BURGER-BITS

¼ pound blue cheese
 1 pound ground beef

½ teaspoon salt
Dash of pepper

Preheat oven to 400°. Cut blue cheese into ½-inch cubes. Season beef with salt and pepper. Wrap enough meat around each cheese cube to cover completely. Place on cookie sheet and bake until nicely browned. Serve hot.
Yield: 25 burger-bits.

CHAMPAGNE DIP

2 tablespoons butter
2 cups grated Gruyere cheese

¼ cup champagne
Dash of salt

Melt butter in blazer of chafing dish over hot water. Add cheese, a little at a time. As cheese melts, gradually stir in champagne. Season with salt. Serve with crusty French bread.
Yield: about 2¼ cups.

CHEESE AND BEER SPREAD

 2 cups grated sharp Cheddar cheese
¼ cup beer
 2 tablespoons butter, softened
½ teaspoon prepared mustard

Dash of cayenne
1 tablespoon chopped chives
2 teaspoons chopped pimiento

Combine all ingredients except the chives and pimiento. Mix well. Add chives and pimiento. Serve spread on rye rounds.
Yield: about 1¾ cups.

COCKTAIL CRISPIES

 2 cups grated sharp Cheddar cheese
½ cup butter, softened

1 cup sifted all-purpose flour
¼ teaspoon salt

Preheat oven to 425°. Combine all ingredients and mix well. Roll into marble size balls. Place 1-inch apart on cookie sheet and bake 12 to 15 minutes.
Yield: 4 to 5 dozen.

DEVILED-HAM PINEAPPLE DIP

1 4½-oz. can deviled ham
1 3-oz. package cream cheese, softened
¾ cup crushed pineapple, drained

Combine ham and cream cheese. Add crushed pineapple and just enough pineapple juice to make a dipping consistency. Serve with cocktail tidbits.
Yield: about 2½ cups.

FAMILY FARE CHEESE BALL

1 8-oz. package cream cheese, softened
1 cup finely chopped cooked turkey
¾ cup finely chopped toasted almonds
⅓ cup mayonnaise
2 tablespoons chopped chutney
1 tablespoon curry powder
¼ teaspoon salt
Chopped fresh parsley

Combine all ingredients except the parsley. Mix well. Chill. Shape into a ball. Roll in chopped parsley.
Yield: about 3 cups.

OLIVE AND CHEESE ROUNDS

1 cup grated American cheese
3 tablespoons butter, softened
½ cup all-purpose flour
¼ teaspoon salt
½ teaspoon paprika
2 7-oz. jars Spanish olives

Preheat oven to 400°. Combine cheese and butter. Stir in flour, salt, and paprika. Wrap enough dough around each olive to cover completely. Bake 10 to 15 minutes. Serve hot.
Yield: about 25 cheese rounds.

THE ROAD PARTY DIP

1 8-oz. package cream cheese,
  softened
1½ cups crabmeat, flaked
2 tablespoons finely chopped onion
2 tablespoons milk
½ teaspoon prepared horseradish
¼ teaspoon salt
Dash of pepper
⅓ cup slivered toasted almonds

Combine all ingredients except almonds. Mix well. Pour into casserole dish. Sprinkle with almonds. Bake 15 minutes at 375°. Serve with breadsticks, melba toast, or crackers.
Yield: about 2½ cups.

SESAME CHEESE LOG

¼ cup sesame seeds
1 8-oz. package cream cheese,
  softened
1 4-oz. package blue cheese,
  crumbled
½ cup soft butter
½ cup chopped, pitted, green olives
2 tablespoons Worcestershire sauce
1 tablespoon chopped chives
1 tablespoon chopped fresh parsley

Spread sesame seeds in a shallow baking pan. Bake 8 to 10 minutes at 375°. Toss occasionally. Combine cream cheese and blue cheese. Mix well. Add remaining ingredients, except sesame seeds. Chill. Form into a log 2½-inches in diameter. Roll in sesame seeds.
Yield: about 2½ cups.

SOUPS

There are certain days when soup seems to be the perfect thing to serve. Try one of these cheese soups for variety and good taste. Be prepared to refill the soup bowl!

Soups always seem to be enhanced when served with crackers or croutons of all sizes and flavors. Spread the crackers or croutons with melted butter, then sprinkle with grated Parmesan cheese, heat in the oven 10 minutes at 350°. Or cut bread into thin strips, spread with melted butter, toast in the oven, then cover with grated Parmesan cheese, and broil until cheese melts.

You can also add variety to some soups with the addition of cheese. For instance, try melting grated Cheddar cheese in a seafood soup, or sprinkling grated cheese over a cream soup, or floating a cream cheese ball, which has been rolled in minced chives, in a steaming bowl of tomato soup.

AFTER THE GAME SOUP

1 small carrot, grated	3 cups milk
¼ cup chopped onion	2 cups grated American cheese
¼ cup butter	½ cup beer
¼ cup all-purpose flour	Salt and pepper to taste

Sauté carrots and onion in melted butter until soft. Gradually stir in flour. Slowly add milk, stirring constantly. Cook until thickened. Add cheese, a little at a time, stirring until melted. Blend in beer. Salt and pepper to taste. Heat; do not boil.
Yield: 4 to 6 servings.

ALPINE ONION SOUP

4 large onions	1 tablespoon Worcestershire sauce
½ cup butter	1 loaf French bread
3 10½-oz. cans condensed beef broth	¼ cup grated Parmesan cheese
	¼ cup grated Swiss cheese
1¼ cups water	Butter
2 tablespoons dry white wine	

Peel and thinly slice onions. In a large saucepan sauté onions in melted butter over low heat for 30 minutes or until soft. Stir often. Add broth, water, wine, and Worcestershire. Bring to a boil. Lower heat, cover and simmer 30 minutes. Preheat oven to 350°. Cut bread into 1½-inch thick slices and place on cookie sheet. Toast 20 minutes. Pour soup into shallow baking dish; then place toast on top. Combine cheeses and sprinkle over bread. Dot with butter. Bake 5 to 8 minutes at 400° or until cheese melts.
Yield: 6 servings.

BUBBLY-BROCCOLI SOUP

1 small onion, finely chopped	2 cups milk
2 tablespoons butter	1½ cups grated Cheddar cheese
3 tablespoons all-purpose flour	1½ cups chicken stock
½ teaspoon salt	1 10-oz. package frozen broccoli, cooked and drained
⅛ teaspoon pepper	

Sauté onions in melted butter until soft. Gradually stir in flour, salt, and pepper. Slowly add milk, stirring constantly. Cook until thickened. Add cheese, a little at a time, stirring until melted. Remove from heat. Stir in chicken stock and cooked broccoli; heat.
Yield: 4 to 6 servings.

HEART-WARMING SOUP

1 small onion, finely chopped
¼ cup grated carrot
¼ cup butter
⅓ cup all-purpose flour

1 teaspoon salt
Dash of pepper
4 cups milk
2 cups grated American cheese

Sauté onions and carrots in melted butter until soft. Gradually stir in flour, salt, and pepper. Slowly add milk, stirring constantly. Cook until thickened. Add cheese, a little at a time, stirring until melted.
Yield: 4 to 6 servings.

POTATO CHEESE SOUP

3 medium potatoes
1 13-oz. can concentrated chicken broth
⅓ cup butter
¼ cup all-purpose flour
1 14½-oz. can evaporated milk
1 can water
1 1-pound can kernel corn, with liquid

1 1-pound can green beans, with liquid
1 medium onion
1 2-oz. jar pimiento, diced
¼ teaspoon pepper
1 bay leaf
¾ cup cubed Cheddar cheese
8 hard cooked eggs, sliced
Salt and pepper to taste

Peel and cut potatoes into 1-inch cubes; then simmer in chicken broth, covered, 10 minutes or until just tender. Melt butter in a large saucepan, stir in flour. Dilute evaporated milk with water; then pour into saucepan. Cook, stirring constantly, until smooth and thickened. Add corn, beans, onion, pimiento, pepper, bay leaf, potatoes, and broth. Simmer 15 minutes. Remove bay leaf. Before serving add cheese and eggs. Season to taste.
Yield: 6 to 8 servings.

WINE AND CHEESE SOUP

½ cup dry white wine

⅛ teaspoon garlic powder

1 cup grated Swiss cheese
¼ teaspoon nutmeg
⅛ teaspoon pepper

1 cup light cream
1 10½-oz. can condensed cream
  of celery soup

Combine ingredients. Heat in double boiler over simmering water.
Yield: 6 servings.

SALADS AND DRESSINGS

Salads have become an important part of most meals. They may be the crisp counterpart to a meal or even, nowadays, the meal itself.

And cheese dressings, in their many varieties, will make an everyday salad "an experience."

Another thing to keep in mind is the nutritional value of a cheese salad or a cheese dressing. The use of fresh vegetables and the use of cheese makes a potent nutritional combination. Add a crumbly cheese, such as blue, into a salad for added taste, texture, and nutrition.

BEAN SALAD

2 cups dried pea beans
6 cups boiling water
1 small onion, thinly sliced
1 medium cucumber, peeled and
  chopped

½ cup olive oil
¼ cup lemon juice
2 garlic cloves, crushed
1 teaspoon salt
¾ cup crumbled feta cheese

Cook beans in boiling water for 2 minutes. Remove from heat. Cover and let stand 1 hour. Again bring to a boil. Cook until tender. Drain. Chill. Combine beans with remaining ingredients. Chill. Toss occasionally.
Yield: 4 to 6 servings.

BRUNCH COLESLAW

4 cups shredded cabbage
1 tomato, chopped
1 cup cubed Cheddar cheese
½ cup sliced celery

¼ cup chopped onion
¼ cup radish slices
Prepared salad dressing

Combine ingredients except for salad dressing. Toss salad with enough dressing to moisten. Chill.
Yield: 4 to 6 servings.

EASY FIX-IT SALAD

2 cups cottage cheese
½ cup dairy sour cream
¼ cup chopped chives

½ cup cucumber, peeled and diced
1 tablespoon watercress
Salt and pepper to taste

Combine ingredients. Shape into mounds. Serve each portion on a bed of lettuce leaves.
Yield: 4 servings.

FREEZE-A-SALAD

⅔ cup evaporated milk
1 tablespoon fresh lemon juice
1 8-oz. package cream cheese, softened
⅓ cup mayonnaise

1 8¾-oz. can crushed pineapple drained
½ cup sliced dates
½ cup chopped walnuts
¼ cup chopped maraschino cherries

Chill evaporated milk; then whip until stiff peaks form. Mix in lemon juice. Cream cheese until smooth. Blend in mayonnaise. Stir in fruit. Fold cream cheese mixture into whipped evaporated milk. Spoon into 9-inch square pan or into eight ¾ cup molds. Cover. Freeze.
Yield: 8 servings.

1 cup heavy cream
¼ cup honey
1 8-oz. package cream cheese, softened

2 10-oz. packages frozen blueberries, thawed

Whip cream until stiff. Slowly add honey to cream cheese. Mix well. Add and stir in blueberries. Fold in whipped cream. Spoon into 9-inch square pan or eight ¾ cup molds. Cover. Freeze.
Yield: 8 servings.

LUNCHEON CHEESE RING

1 6-oz. package lemon-flavored
  gelatin
3 cups tomato juice, hot
¾ cup mayonnaise

2 3-oz. packages cream cheese,
  softened
3 hard-cooked eggs, chopped
½ cup sliced stuffed olives

Dissolve gelatin in hot tomato juice. Chill. Beat mayonnaise and cream cheese until smooth and well blended. Add gelatin mixture; beat until well blended. Chill until just thickened but not set. Fold in eggs and olives. Pour into 1½-quart ring mold; chill until firm. Unmold on crisp lettuce.
Yield: 8 servings.

REGAL CHICKEN SALAD

1 tablespoon lemon juice
2 tart apples, chopped
4 cups finely chopped cooked chicken
1 celery stalk, chopped
1 cup green grapes, cut in half
¾ cup mayonnaise

½ teaspoon salt
¼ teaspoon pepper
1 8-oz. package cream cheese,
  softened
¼ cup mayonnaise

In a 1½-quart bowl, toss lemon juice with apples to coat. Mix in chicken, celery, grapes, mayonnaise and seasonings. Press into bowl. Chill 3 to 4 hours. Unmold on serving dish. Combine cream cheese and mayonnaise. Mix until well blended. Frost chicken salad.
Yield: 8 servings.

SUPPER SALAD

5 medium potatoes, cooked, peeled
  and cut in cubes
1¼ cups milk
1 8-oz. package cream cheese,
  softened

1 tablespoon chopped fresh chives
¼ teaspoon salt

In a saucepan, combine milk and cream cheese. Simmer, stirring constantly, until well blended. Remove from heat. Stir in chives, salt, and potatoes. Mix carefully to coat. Pour into a baking dish. Bake 30 minutes at 350°.
Yield: 4 servings.

TEMPTY POTATO SALAD

4 potatoes, peeled, cooked, and
  diced
2 small zucchini, diced
½ pound sliced fresh mushrooms
1 firm tomato, diced
¼ cup chopped onions
½ cup olive oil

2 tablespoons Worcestershire sauce
4 teaspoons fresh lemon juice
1¼ teaspoons salt
1 small clove garlic, crushed
¼ teaspoon pepper
¼ teaspoon oregano leaves
¾ cup grated Parmesan cheese

Combine potatoes, zucchini, mushrooms, tomato, and onion. Combine remaining ingredients, except cheese; mix well. Pour over vegetables; toss to coat. Chill. Just before serving, sprinkle with grated cheese.
Yield: 4 to 6 servings.

TOSSED VEGETABLE SALAD

1 small head romaine lettuce
2 medium cucumbers, thinly sliced
1 bunch small radishes, thinly sliced
2 small onions, thinly sliced
2 firm tomatoes, cut in wedges
1 cup pitted black olives

⅓ cup olive oil
¼ cup red wine vinegar
1 teaspoon garlic salt
1 teaspoon oregano
½ pound feta cheese, sliced
1 2-oz. can anchovies

Tear romaine into bite-size pieces. Toss gently with cucumbers, radishes, onions, tomatoes, and olives. Combine olive oil, vinegar, salt, and oregano. Pour over salad. Toss to mix. Top with cheese slices and anchovy fillets.
Yield: 4 to 6 servings.

YELLOW-SALAD MOLD

1 3-oz. package lemon-flavored
  gelatin
1½ cups boiling water
1 tablespoon vinegar

1 teaspoon salt
Dash of cayenne
1 cup grated American cheese
½ cup mayonnaise

Dissolve gelatin in boiling water. Add vinegar, salt, and cayenne. Chill. When slightly thickened, beat until consistency of whipped cream. Combine cheese and mayonnaise. Fold into gelatin. Pour into 1-quart mold; chill until firm. Unmold on crisp lettuce.
Yield: 4 to 6 servings.

CALIFORNIA DRESSING

1 3-oz. package cream cheese,
  softened
⅓ cup bottled green goddess
  dressing

1 teaspoon grated orange rind
2 teaspoons lemon juice

Combine ingredients. Mix well. Chill. Serve over crisp lettuce.
Yield: about 1 cup.

CREAMY BLUE CHEESE DRESSING

¼ cup crumbled blue cheese
¼ cup milk
 1 teaspoon Worcestershire sauce
¾ cup mayonnaise

⅛ teaspoon salt
⅛ teaspoon garlic powder
⅛ teaspoon pepper

Combine ingredients; then chill. Serve on salad greens.
Yield: 1 cup.

EMERALD FRUIT DRESSING

½ cup small curd creamed cottage
  cheese
2 tablespoons milk
1 tablespoon sugar

½ teaspoon grated lime rind
1 tablespoon lime juice
½ cup mayonnaise

Combine ingredients. Mix well. Serve on fresh or canned fruit salad.
Yield: 1 cup.

GRANA CHEESE DRESSING

⅓ cup grated Parmesan cheese
⅓ cup milk
⅔ cup mayonnaise

1 teaspoon wine vinegar
¼ teaspoon Worcestershire sauce

Combine ingredients. Mix well. Chill. Serve on tossed green salad.
Yield: 1 cup.

RIVIERA DRESSING

½ cup crumbled Roquefort cheese
¾ cup sour cream
3 tablespoons light cream
1 teaspoon lemon juice
1 teaspoon sugar

1 teaspoon minced onion
½ teaspoon salt
⅛ teaspoon pepper
½ teaspoon chopped fresh parsley

Combine ingredients. Mix well. Chill, preferably overnight.
Yield: 1½ cups.

SHERRY CHEESE DRESSING

2 tablespoons sugar
1 tablespoon lemon juice
1 3-oz. package cream cheese,
  softened

2 tablespoons sherry
Dash salt
¼ cup toasted blanched slivered
  almonds

Gradually stir sugar and lemon juice into softened cream cheese. Stir in sherry, salt, and almonds. Chill. Serve over fresh or canned fruit salads.
Yield: ¾ cup.

QUICK CHEESE DRESSING

1 cup mayonnaise
¼ cup catsup

2 tablespoons chili sauce
½ cup grated Cheddar cheese

Combine mayonnaise, catsup, and chili sauce. Stir in cheese. Chill. Serve on crisp lettuce cups.
Yield: 1⅔ cups.

MAIN DISHES

Meat, meatless, or vegetable dishes bubbling with the goodness of cheese are not only nutritional, substantial, and good, but most of them are great for "thrift" days.

There's something nice and "down to earth" about cheese that makes cooking with it fun, but remember that overcooked cheese becomes tough and stringy.

For recipes calling for grated cheese, it is best to grate your own cheese just before using to preserve its flavor.

CHICKEN-PORK BAKE

1 pound boneless, lean pork, cut
  in 2" strips
2 cups white chicken meat, cut in
  2" strips
¼ cup butter, melted
1½ cups apple juice
1 teaspoon salt

¼ teaspoon rosemary
¼ teaspoon mace
½ cup grated Swiss cheese
½ cup sliced Macadamia nuts
¼ cup chopped pimiento
1 cup sour cream

Noodle cups:
2½ cups chow mein noodles
1 cup grated Cheddar cheese
1 egg white

In a large skillet, brown pork and chicken in melted butter. Add apple juice, salt, rosemary, and mace. Simmer 45 minutes, or until meat is tender. Stir in Swiss cheese, nuts, and pimiento. Simmer, stirring, until cheese melts. Stir in sour cream. Heat, but do not allow to come to a boil. Serve in noodle cups.
Yield: 6 servings.

Noodle cups:
Preheat oven to 300°. Combine ingredients. Mix thoroughly. Press firmly into bottom and sides of 6 buttered muffin tins. Bake 12-15 minutes.

STOWE BRUNCH

½ cup chopped celery
1 tablespoon finely chopped onion
2 tablespoons chicken broth
2 cups cooked, diced chicken
2 teaspoons lemon juice
⅓ teaspoon poultry seasoning

½ teaspoon salt
⅓ cup mayonnaise
6 slices bread
1 tablespoon butter
¾ cup grated Cheddar cheese

Cook celery and onion in chicken broth 10 minutes, in covered pan. Combine chicken, celery and onion mixture, lemon juice, poultry seasoning, salt, and

mayonnaise. Blend well. Preheat broiler. Toast bread on one side under broiler. Butter untoasted side of bread. Spread the chicken mixture on the untoasted side of bread slices. Cover to edges of slices. Sprinkle with cheese; broil until cheese is melted.
Yield: 4 to 6 servings.

BEEF PIE

½ pound ground beef
½ cup mayonnaise
½ cup milk
2 eggs
1 tablespoon cornstarch

1½ cups chopped Swiss cheese
½ cup chopped onion
Dash of pepper
1 9-inch unbaked pastry shell

In a skillet, brown beef over medium heat. Drain fat as it accumulates. In a mixing bowl, combine mayonnaise, milk, eggs, and cornstarch. Mix well. Add browned meat, cheese, onion, and pepper. Pour into pastry shell. Bake 35 to 40 minutes at 350° or until golden.
Yield: 6 servings.

CHILI-CHEESE BAKE

⅓ cup chopped onion
1 garlic clove, sliced
2 tablespoons bacon fat
½ pound ground beef
2½ cups cooked pinto beans
⅓ cup minced green pepper

2½ cups cooked tomatoes
1 bay leaf, crushed
2 teaspoons sugar
3 teaspoons chili powder
Salt and pepper to taste
¾ cup grated Cheddar cheese

Saute onion and garlic in heated bacon fat until soft. Stir in beef. Cook slowly, stirring occasionally, until meat is browned. Mix in remaining ingredients, except cheese. Place mixture in baking dish; then sprinkle with cheese. Bake, uncovered, 30 minutes at 350°.
Yield: 4 servings.

SOPHISTICATED MEATLOAF

2 pounds ground beef
½ cup Italian styled bread crumbs
1 large onion, finely chopped

1 tablespoon butter
2 tablespoons chopped green pepper
1 cup cooked rice

1 8-oz. can tomato sauce
2 eggs
3 teaspoons Worcestershire sauce
1¾ teaspoons salt

½ cup chopped tomato
⅓ cup grated American cheese
1 tablespoon chopped, pitted green olives

In a large bowl, combine beef, bread crumbs, ¾ cup onion, tomato sauce, 1 egg, 2 teaspoon Worcestershire sauce, and 1 teaspoon salt. Mix well. Place ¾ of the mixture into a 9 x 5 x 3-inch loaf pan. Pat to fit bottom and sides of pan. Make a well in the center. Melt butter in a skillet. Sauté remaining onion and green pepper until soft; then stir in rice, 1 egg, 1 teaspoon Worcestershire sauce, and ¾ teaspoon salt. Mix well. Blend in remaining ingredients. Spoon rice mixture into well of meatloaf; then top with remaining meat. Preheat oven to 350°. Bake 1½ hours. Remove from oven, let rest 10 minutes then turn out on serving plate. *Yield 6 to 8 servings.*

STUFFED MANICOTTI

½ 8-oz. package manicotti
3 tablespoons olive oil
1 pound ground beef
½ cup chopped onion
2 garlic cloves, minced
3 6-oz. cans tomato paste

3 cups water
1½ teaspoons salt
Dash of pepper
2 tablespoons chopped fresh parsley
3 teaspoons basil
Grated Parmesan cheese for topping

Filling:
2 cups cream-style cottage cheese
⅓ cup Parmesan cheese
1 egg, beaten

¼ teaspoon salt
Dash of pepper

Cook manicotti according to package directions. Drain. Cool. In a skillet, brown meat in olive oil. Add onion, garlic, tomato paste, water, and seasonings. Simmer, uncovered, until thickened, about 45 minutes. Combine ingredients for filling. Stuff each cooked manicotti with cheese filling. Spoon ½ of the sauce into a baking dish. Arrange stuffed manicotti in a layer, overlapping slightly on sauce. Top with remaining sauce. Sprinkle generously with Parmesan cheese. Bake 25-30 minutes at 350° or until bubbling hot. *Yield: 6 servings.*

A WESTERN FAVORITE

½ pound link sausage, sliced

2 8-oz. cans tomato sauce

1½ pounds ground beef
1 large onion, chopped
1 tablespoon chili powder
2 teaspoons salt
¼ teaspoon pepper
1 12-oz. can whole kernel corn, drained

1 cup milk
½ cup cornmeal
1 small can pitted ripe olives, drained
1 cup grated American cheese

In a large skillet, brown sausage slowly. Pour off fat. Add beef and onion. Cook, stirring, until meat is browned. Add seasonings, corn, tomato sauce, and milk. Simmer 20 minutes. Gradually stir in cornmeal. Add olives. Pour into a baking dish and sprinkle with cheese. Bake 40 minutes at 325°.
Yield: 6 to 8 servings.

HAM AND CHEESE SNACKS

3 cups hot cooked rice
3 tablespoons butter
1 egg, beaten
¼ cup pickle relish
1 tablespoon chopped fresh parsley

8 slices boiled ham
8 slices American cheese
16 very thin onion slices
8 slices tomato
2 tablespoons grated Parmesan cheese

In a mixing bowl, combine hot rice and butter. Stir in egg, pickle relish, and parsley. Mix well. Grease a 15½ x 10½ inch sheet pan. Spoon mixture into pan and spread evenly. Bake 10 minutes at 350°. Meanwhile, cut ham and American cheese into 4 x 4-inch squares. Arrange ham, cheese, onion, and tomato slices in eight stacks. Sprinkle with Parmesan cheese. Arrange stacks on baked rice. Make sure all the rice is covered. Preheat broiler. Broil just long enough to melt cheese. Cut into squares and serve immediately.
Yield: 8 servings.

OLD-WORLD NOODLE BAKE

1 8-oz. package broad egg noodles
8 slices bacon
1 large onion, chopped
2 tablespoons butter
2 eggs, beaten

1 teaspoon salt
½ teaspoon nutmeg
2 cups diced Swiss cheese
½ cup grated Parmesan cheese

Cook noodles according to package directions. Drain. Fry bacon until crisp. In a small skillet, sauté onions in butter until soft. In a mixing bowl, combine eggs,

salt, and nutmeg. Stir in noodles, onions, crumbled bacon, and cheese. Pour into a baking dish. Bake 45 minutes at 375° or until golden.
Yield: 10 to 12 servings.

ZESTY SAUSAGE-CHEESE BOATS

4 medium zucchini	**1 egg, slightly beaten**
¼ pound bulk pork sausage	**½ teaspoon monosodium glutamate**
1 small onion, chopped	**¼ teaspoon salt**
½ cup grated Parmesan cheese	**¼ teaspoon thyme**
½ cup fine cracker crumbs	**Garlic salt and pepper to taste**

Cook whole zucchini in small amount of boiling water 7 to 10 minutes, or until barely tender. Cool. Cut in half lengthwise; scoop squash from shells and mash. In a skillet, cook sausage and onion. Drain off excess fat. Stir in mashed zucchini. Set aside 2 tablespoons cheese. Stir remaining ingredients and cheese into skillet. Spoon mixture into zucchini shells; place in shallow baking dish. Sprinkle with remaining cheese. Bake 25 to 30 minutes at 350°.
Yield: 4 servings.

ALMOND STUDDED FILLETS

2 tablespoons butter	**½ cup grated American cheese**
2 tablespoons all-purpose flour	**1 tablespoon sherry**
¼ teaspoon salt	**1 pound frozen fish fillets**
Dash cayenne	**⅓ cup diced roasted almonds**
1 cup milk	

Melt butter in a saucepan. Blend in flour, salt, and cayenne. Slowly add milk. Cook, stirring, until thickened. Blend in cheese and wine. Stir over very low heat until cheese is melted. Place fish fillets in shallow baking dish. Cover with hot sauce and bake 20 minutes at 400°. Sprinkle with almonds and serve at once.
Yield: 4 servings.

FISHERMAN'S DELIGHT

1½ pounds mixed seafood (scallops, halibut, sole or flounder fillets)	**1 ¾-oz. package white sauce mix**
1 4-oz. can mushrooms, sliced	**1¼ cups milk**
¼ cup white wine	**2 tablespoons grated Parmesan cheese**

2 tablespoons finely chopped onion
1 tablespoon Worcestershire sauce
⅛ teaspoon salt

2 tablespoons pimiento, diced
2 tablespoons parsley flakes
½ cup buttered bread crumbs

Wash and drain fish; set aside. Drain mushrooms. Add sufficient water to mushroom liquid to measure 1 cup. In a saucepan, combine mushroom liquid, wine, onion, Worcestershire, and salt. Bring to a boil. Add seafood. Simmer until it just flakes. Remove fish from pan with a slotted spoon. Cut into chunks; set aside. Stir white sauce mix, milk, and cheese into liquid remaining in pot. Cook, stirring constantly, until thickened. Stir in seafood, mushrooms, parsley, and pimiento. Simmer 5 minutes. Turn into a baking dish. Sprinkle with buttered bread crumbs. Bake 10 minutes at 400° or until bubbly.
Yield: 6 servings.

GREAT LOBSTER THERMIDOR

4 cooked lobster tails
3 tablespoons butter
1 tablespoon instant minced onion
¼ cup white wine
3 tablespoons all-purpose flour
2 cups light cream
1 tablespoon chopped fresh parsley

¾ teaspoon salt
¼ teaspoon dry mustard
Dash cayenne
¼ cup diced roasted almonds
1 cup grated Cheddar cheese
Paprika

Cut meat from lobster tails. Set aside. In a saucepan, melt butter. Add onion and wine and simmer until liquid is reduced to half. Add flour; stir until smooth. Slowly add cream, continue to cook, stirring until thickened and creamy. Add parsley, salt, mustard, and cayenne. Fold in cubed lobster, almonds, and ½ cup cheese. Stir until cheese is melted. Fill lobster tails with mixture or place in 4 individual casseroles. Sprinkle with remaining cheese and paprika. Broil until cheese melts, about 2 minutes.
Yield: 4 servings.

MARITIME CHEESE BAKE*

2 cups cottage cheese
1 7-oz. can tuna fish
¼ cup dry bread crumbs
2 eggs, beaten
½ teaspoon salt

¼ teaspoon pepper
¾ teaspoon celery salt
Dash of steak sauce
¼ cup buttered bread crumbs

Combine cheese, tuna, ¼ cup bread crumbs, and seasonings; then blend into beaten egg. Place in greased baking dish. Sprinkle with buttered bread crumbs. Set in pan of hot water. Bake 30 minutes at 375° or until mixture is firm. *Yield: 4 servings.*

*A low-calorie dish: approximately 375 calories per serving.

SEAFARING CASSEROLE

1 4-oz. can mushrooms, drained, sliced	3 tablespoons fresh lemon juice
2 tablespoons butter, melted	¼ teaspoon salt
¼ cup all-purpose flour	2½ cups cooked shrimp
1½ cups milk	1 cup cooked crabmeat
1 cup grated Cheddar cheese	1 7½-oz. can clams, drained, minced
3 tablespoons chili sauce	

Brown mushrooms in melted butter. Blend in flour. Slowly add milk, stirring constantly. Simmer until thickened. Remove from heat. Add cheese, a little at a time. Stir until melted. Blend in chili sauce, lemon juice, salt, shrimp, crabmeat, and clams. Heat. Serve over toast or rice. *Yield: 6 servings.*

MEATLESS AND VEGETABLE DISHES

ALPINE RICE

2 tablespoons butter	⅓ cup grated Swiss cheese
4 cups hot cooked rice	½ cup heavy cream
⅓ cup grated Parmesan cheese	

Melt butter; then combine with rice and cheese. Mix well. Heat heavy cream. Pour over mixture. Mix lightly. Serve at once. *Yield: 6 servings.*

ARTICHOKE CASSEROLE

4 large artichokes
1 teaspoon salt
1 7-oz. can tuna fish
¼ cup butter

¼ cup all-purpose flour
1¾ cups milk
⅛ teaspoon curry powder
⅓ cup grated American cheese

Wash artichokes, trim off stems. Turn upside down and press stem ends firmly to spread leaves. Place in pan with 1'' boiling water and salt. Cover. Cook 30 to 45 minutes or until tender. Drain. Pull off leaves. Scrape off and reserve edible portion of each leaf. Remove fuzzy choke. Place hearts in shallow baking dish. Drain oil from tuna. Coarsely flake; then place between artichoke hearts. In a saucepan, melt butter; stir in flour. Slowly add milk and cook, stirring until thickened. Stir in curry powder and artichoke pulp. Spoon mixture over artichokes and tuna. Sprinkle with cheese. Bake 15 to 20 minutes at 350° or until cheese is melted.
Yield: 4 servings.

BAKED OKRA WITH TOMATO SAUCE

1 pound fresh okra
1 medium onion, chopped
1 tablespoon fresh minced parsley
2 tablespoons butter, melted

½ teaspoon salt
¼ teaspoon pepper
 1 cup tomato sauce
¼ cup grated provolone cheese

Cut off stems, wash, and slice okra. Sauté onion and parsley in melted butter 3 minutes. Season with salt and pepper; then arrange in baking dish. Pour tomato sauce over all. Bake 20 minutes at 300°. Sprinkle with grated cheese; then bake 10 minutes longer.
Yield: 6 servings.

BEANS IN CHEESE SAUCE

1 tablespoon butter
1 tablespoon all-purpose flour
1 cup milk
1 teaspoon Worcestershire sauce

½ teaspoon salt
 1 cup grated sharp Cheddar cheese
 3 cups cooked kidney beans

Melt butter in a skillet. Stir in flour until mixture is smooth. Slowly add milk. Cook over very low heat, stirring constantly, until mixture thickens. Add Worces-

tershire sauce, salt, and cheese; stir until cheese melts. Add beans. Place over low heat and heat thoroughly.
Yield: 4 servings.

BROCCOLI-CHEESE SOUFFLE

¼ cup quick-cooking tapioca	4 egg yolks
1 teaspoon salt	½ teaspoon marjoram
1⅓ cups milk	1 cup cooked, chopped broccoli
1 cup grated Cheddar cheese	4 egg whites

In a saucepan, combine tapioca, salt, and milk. Cook over medium heat, stirring, until mixture comes to a boil. Remove from heat. Add cheese. Stir until melted. In a large mixing bowl, beat egg yolks until thick. Add tapioca mixture, marjoram, and broccoli. Mix well. Beat egg whites until stiff but not dry; then fold into cheese mixture. Pour into a 1½-quart baking dish; set in a pan of hot water. Bake 1 hour at 325° or until a knife inserted in center comes out clean.
Yield: 6 servings.

CHEESE PIE

½ pound feta cheese, crumbled	1 tablespoon fresh or dry dill
1 16-oz. carton cottage cheese (or pot cheese)	½ teaspoon salt
1 cup grated Parmesan cheese	6 eggs
½ pound butter, melted	1 pound butter, melted
1 tablespoon fresh chopped parsley	1 pound strudel sheets

Combine cheeses. Stir in ½ pound melted butter, parsley, dill, and salt. Add eggs, one at a time. Mix well. Butter a 10 x 14 x 2-inch pan. Lay in 6 strudel sheets, brushing each sheet with melted butter. Spread mixture over pastry. Cover with remaining pastry, brushing each sheet with melted butter. Fold in edges to hold in mixture. With a sharp knife, lightly cut 2-inch squares through the top layer of pastry only. Preheat oven to 350°. Bake 40 to 45 minutes or until golden. Serve hot.
Yield: 8 to 12 servings.

Strudel pastry sheets, also known as "filo," can be found in most specialty food stores, Greek, Austrian, or German groceries. It is sold in 1 pound boxes in the refrigerated section.

Because strudel sheets dry rapidly when exposed to air, it is best to work quickly. When the sheets are removed from the container, cover with a dampened towel.

Pastry sheets may be frozen and will keep from 2 to 3 months. Thaw at room temperature before using.

EGGPLANT WITH TOMATOES*

2 cups cooked, chopped eggplant
1 cup cooked tomatoes
2 tablespoons butter

Salt and pepper to taste
¼ cup bread crumbs
2 tablespoons Parmesan cheese

Butter a baking dish. Cover bottom with a layer of eggplant; then cover eggplant with a layer of tomatoes. Dot with butter. Season with salt and pepper. Repeat until all ingredients are used. Combine bread crumbs and cheese. Sprinkle over top. Bake 20 minutes at 350°.
Yield: 4 servings.

*A low-calorie dish: approximately 185 calories per serving.

EGGS OVER ASPARAGUS

1½ pound asparagus
  2 tablespoons vegetable oil
  1 garlic clove

4 eggs
Salt and pepper to taste
½ cup grated Romano cheese

Wash asparagus. Cut stalks as far down as they break easily. Cook upright in 1-inch boiling, salted water 10 to 20 minutes. Peel; then cut garlic in half. Sauté in hot oil for 1 minute. Remove from skillet. Fry eggs in skillet, covered, 3 minutes, or until eggs are cooked as preferred. Season to taste. Divide asparagus into four serving portions; place an egg on each portion. Sprinkle with cheese.
Yield: 4 servings.

HEARTY CHEESE CHILE

1 medium onion, thinly sliced
2 tablespoons butter
1 garlic clove, minced
2 tablespoons chili powder
2 16-oz. canned tomatoes, mashed

3 cups pinto beans
Salt and pepper to taste
1½ cups grated Cheddar cheese
3 cups hot cooked rice

Sauté onion in butter until soft but not brown. Stir in garlic and chili powder. Add tomatoes, beans, salt, and pepper. Simmer 10 minutes. Add cheese. Cook until cheese melts, stirring constantly. Spoon mixture into individual soup bowl. Top with mounds of rice.
Yield: 6 servings.

HEAVENLY CARROTS

1 pound carrots
2 eggs, beaten
1½ cups milk
1 cup grated colby cheese

1 cup seasoned bread crumbs
2 tablespoons butter, softened
Salt and pepper to taste

Scrub carrots well. Cook, covered, in 1-inch boiling salted water 15 to 20 minutes. Drain. Mash. Combine carrots and remaining ingredients. Mix well. Turn into a baking dish. Bake 30 minutes at 350°, or until a knife inserted just off-center comes out clean.
Yield: 4 to 6 servings.

MUSHROOM-CHEESE BAKE

3 tablespoons butter
2 tablespoons all-purpose flour
1 cup milk
½ teaspoon salt
⅛ teaspoon pepper
1½ pounds mushrooms, washed
and sliced

1 small onion, chopped
2 tablespoons pimiento, cut into
strips
1 tablespoon chopped fresh mint
¼ teaspoon dry mustard
1 cup grated Cheddar cheese
¼ cup buttered bread crumbs

In a saucepan melt 2 tablespoons butter. Stir in flour. Slowly add milk, stirring, until mixture thickens. Cook 3 minutes longer. Season with salt and pepper. In a skillet, sauté mushrooms in 1 tablespoon butter. Combine mushrooms, onions, pimiento, mint, and mustard with sauce mixture. Pour into a greased baking dish. Sprinkle with cheese and bread crumbs. Bake 10 to 15 minutes at 375° or until cheese melts.
Yield: 6 servings.

RICE WITH CHEESE

¼ cup all-purpose flour

½ cup chopped fresh parsley

1 teaspoon salt
¹₈ teaspoon pepper
½ teaspoon dry summer savory
2 tablespoons minced onion

3 cups cooked rice
2 cups grated American cheese
2 cups light cream
Paprika

Combine flour, salt, pepper, summer savory, onion, and parsley. Stir in rice and 1 cup cheese. Pour mixture into a buttered 2-quart casserole. Pour in cream: top with remaining cheese. Sprinkle with paprika. Bake 40 to 45 minutes at 350°. *Yield: 6 to 8 servings.*

SCALLOPED MUSHROOMS

3 pounds fresh mushrooms
½ cup butter
1 cup heavy cream
½ teaspoon salt

½ teaspoon pepper
¹₈ teaspoon cayenne
2 cups grated Gruyere cheese

Wash mushrooms; then pat dry. Sauté in butter 5 minutes. Add cream and cook till most of liquid disappears. Season with salt, pepper, and cayenne. Spoon into greased baking dish. Bake at 400° just until lightly brown. *Yield: 10 to 12 servings.*

SCALLOPED POTATOES

6 potatoes, thinly sliced
Salt and pepper to taste
4 onions, thinly sliced
4 tablespoons butter

5 slices Swiss cheese, cut in strips
½ cup grated Parmesan cheese
1½ cups milk

Butter a baking dish; then cover bottom with a layer of potatoes. Season with salt and pepper. Layer onions over potatoes; dot with butter. Layer Swiss cheese strips over onions and sprinkle with Parmesian cheese. Repeat, ending with Swiss cheese strips. Pour in enough milk so that it comes up to the level of the mixture. Bake 50 minutes at 350° or until the potatoes are soft. *Yield: 4 to 6 servings.*

SPINACH PIE

1 pound fresh spinach (or 2 10-oz. pkg. frozen leaf spinach, thawed)

3 eggs, beaten
Salt and pepper to taste

2 medium onions, finely chopped
¼ cup olive oil
½ pound feta cheese, crumbled
1 6-oz. carton cottage cheese
  (ricotta or pot cheese)

1 tablespoon minced fresh parsley
½ teaspoon dry dill
½ pound strudel sheets*
½ cup butter, melted

Wash spinach thoroughly. Drain. Dry completely. Chop fine. Sauté onions in oil until soft. In a mixing bowl, combine spinach, feta and cottage cheese, eggs, salt, pepper, parsley, and dill. Stir in onions. Mix well. Butter a 10 x 4 x 2-inch pan. Lay in 6 strudel sheets, brushing each sheet with melted butter. Spread mixture over the pastry. Cover with remaining pastry, brushing each sheet with melted butter. With a sharp knife lightly cut 2'' squares through the top layer of pastry only. Preheat oven to 350°. Bake 35 to 40 minutes or until golden. Serve hot or cold.
Yield: 8 to 12 servings.
*See page 110.

SPINACH RICE FRITTATA

½ cup finely chopped onion
2 tablespoons butter
1½ cups cooked chopped spinach,
  drained
1 garlic clove, crushed
3 cups cooked rice

½ cup grated Parmesan cheese
4 eggs, slightly beaten
½ cup milk
2 teaspoon salt
¼ teaspoon pepper
1 cup grated mozzarella cheese

In a skillet, sauté onions in butter until soft. Add spinach, garlic, rice, and Parmesan cheese. Mix well. Remove from heat. Combine eggs, milk, and seasoning. Stir into skillet. Turn into a shallow 2-quart baking dish. Top with cheese. Bake 30 minutes at 350° or until set.
Yield: 6 servings.

SUMMER SOUFFLE*

4 medium zucchini
2 small onions, finely chopped
3 tablespoons olive oil
4 eggs, beaten
¼ cup Bisquick flour
¼ cup grated Parmesan cheese
1 16-oz container cottage cheese

¼ teaspoon finely chopped fresh
  parsley
¼ teaspoon finely chopped fresh
  dill
Salt and pepper to taste
¼ cup bread crumbs
2 tablespoons butter

Peel; then cut zucchini into cubes. Cook, covered, in small amount of water until soft. Drain, Mash. Sauté onion in oil until soft. In a bowl, combine zucchini and onions. Stir in beaten eggs, flour, Parmesan cheese, cottage cheese, parsley, and dill. Season to taste. Grease a medium-sized baking dish. Dust with bread crumbs. Pour in mixture; top with pieces of butter. Bake 25 minutes at 350° or until firm and fluffy.
Yield: 6 servings.

*A low-calorie dish: approximately 350 calories per serving.

TOMATO RABBIT*

½ cup finely chopped celery
¼ cup chopped green pepper
¼ cup chopped onion
2 tablespoons butter, melted
2 tablespoons all-purpose flour
2½ cups fresh tomatoes, peeled
  and seeded

1 teaspoon salt
1 cup grated Cheddar cheese
2 eggs, beaten
Dash Tabasco sauce (optional)

Cook celery, green pepper, and onion in melted butter 8 to 10 minutes, stirring frequently. Blend in flour. Add tomatoes and salt. Cook slowly until mixture thickens, stirring often. Remove from heat. Add cheese. Stir until cheese melts. Gradually add some of the tomato mixture to beaten eggs; mix well. Stir the egg-tomato mixture into the rest of the tomato mixture. Cook over low heat, stirring constantly, 2 to 3 minutes or until thickened and creamy. If desired, add a few dashes of Tabasco sauce. Serve on toast.
Yield: 6 servings.

*A low-calorie dish: approximately 350 calories per serving.

ZUCCHINI CASSEROLE

1½ pounds zucchini
1 pound ground beef
2 small onions, chopped
1 cup instant rice
1 teaspoon garlic salt

1 teaspoon crushed oregano
2 cups small curd cottage cheese
1 10½-oz. can cream of mushroom
  soup
1 cup grated sharp Cheddar cheese

Peel; then slice zucchini in ¼-inch rounds. Cook, covered, in small amount of boiling salted water until barely tender. Drain. In a skillet, sauté beef with onion until meat is browned. Add rice, salt, garlic and oregano. Place half of the

zucchini in bottom of baking dish. Cover with beef mixture; then cover with cottage cheese. Place remaining zucchini on top and spread soup over all. Sprinkle with Cheddar cheese. Bake, uncovered, 35-40 minutes at 350°.
Yield: 6 to 8 servings.

DESSERTS

Cheese desserts can vary from elegant cheesecakes, souffles, and pies to colorful platters of cheese and fruit.

A plate of cheese and fruit may be less elegant, but there is little likelihood that it will be less loved and enjoyed. Surround slices of juicy tart apples or melon balls with Cheddar or Monterey cheese. Sweet table grapes are fine with Swiss and brick cheese. Or set up a mouth watering platter of succulent pears and apples with Roquefort and provolone cheese. Try a combination of fresh plums and Camembert. A nice platter is a choice of fruit encircled by an assortment of cheese including the bright red-sealed Gouda.

To bring out the natural flavor and texture of a cheese remove from the refrigerator an hour or two before serving. The harder the cheese, the longer it should be allowed to "ripen" at room temperature. Camembert and Brie should be kept in a slightly warmer area so that the soft center will be fairly liquid. However, the unripened cheeses, cream, cottage, and Neufchatel should remain chilled until served.

APPLE PIE

Crust:
1 cup all-purpose flour, sifted
¼ teaspoon salt
2 tablespoons sugar
½ cup butter
¼ pound small curd cottage cheese

Filling:
2 tablespoons dry bread crumbs
6 large apples, peeled, cored, and sliced
1 8-oz. package dates, chopped
½ cup sugar
3 tablespoons all-purpose flour
3 tablespoons butter

Crust:
Sift together flour, salt, and sugar. With a pastry blender, cut in butter until mixture resembles coarse meal. Add cottage cheese. Mix with a fork until a dough

forms. Divide dough in half. Roll bottom crust on a well-floured board. If crust breaks, press together with fingers. Fit into a 9-inch pie pan.

Filling:
Preheat oven to 450°. Sprinkle bottom crust with bread crumbs. Combine apples, dates, sugar, and flour. Mix to coat; then place in pie pan. Dot with butter. Roll remaining dough on well-floured board. Place loosely over filling. Seal edges and prick top crust generously. Bake 10 minutes; lower temperature to 350° and bake 30 more minutes or until crust is golden brown.
Yield: 8 servings.

CHEESE CRUST

⅓ cup boiling water
⅔ cup shortening
2 cups sifted all-purpose flour

¾ teaspoon salt
½ cup grated sharp Cheddar cheese

Pour boiling water over shortening; beat until creamy. Cool. Sift flour with salt. Add flour and cheese to shortening and with a fork mix to a soft dough. Wrap in waxed paper. Chill before rolling.
Yield: 2 crust pie.

CHEESE CUSTARD PUDDING

2 cups cottage cheese
4 eggs
1 quart milk, scalded
3 tablespoons flour

½ teaspoon salt
½ cup sugar
1 teaspoon vanilla extract
¼ teaspoon almond extract

Put cottage cheese through a sieve. Beat eggs together slightly; add scalded milk, stirring to blend. Mix flour, salt, sugar, and sieved cottage cheese. Gradually stir in milk-egg mixture; add vanilla and almond extract. Pour into a well-greased 8-inch glass baking dish; then place in a pan of hot water. Bake 1½ hours at 325° or until a knife inserted in center comes out clean. Cool.
Yield: 6 to 8 servings.

CHEESECAKE MAGNIFIQUE

Crust:
¾ cup crushed Zwieback or graham
   cracker crumbs

1 tablespoon sugar
2 tablespoons butter, melted

Filling:

1 4-oz. package chocolate fudge
  pudding and pie fillling
¾ cup sugar
1 cup milk
1 square unsweetened chocolate
3 8-oz. packages cream cheese,
  softened

3 eggs, separated
2 teaspoons vanilla extract
⅛ teaspoon cinnamon
¼ teaspoon salt

Topping:

1 cup dairy sour cream
¼ cup confectioners' sugar

Crust:

Combine crumbs, sugar, and butter; mix well. Grease sides of a 9-inch
spring-form pan to 1-inch from top. Sprinkle about 2 tablespoons crumb mixture
on sides of pan. Press remaining crumb mixture firmly on bottom of pan.

Filling:

In a saucepan, combine pudding, sugar, and milk. Add chocolate. Cook, stirring,
over medium heat until chocolate is melted and mixture comes to a full boil.
Remove from heat. Cover surface with wax paper. In a large bowl beat cream
cheese until soft and fluffy, using low speed of electric mixer. Add egg yolks; beat
well. Add vanilla, cinnamon, salt, and cooked pudding; blend well. Beat egg
whites until they form soft peaks; fold into cream cheese mixture. Pour over the
crumb mixture in pan. Preheat oven to 425°. Bake 30 minutes, or until center is
set when lightly touched. (cake will become firmer when cooled.)

Topping:

Combine sour cream with confectioners' sugar. Spread over hot cheesecake; then
bake 1 minute at 425° or until shiny, but not brown. Cool to room temperature;
then store in refrigerator.
Yield: 10 to 12 servings.

CHOCOLATE CLOUD SOUFFLE

1 3-oz. package cream cheese
½ cup light cream
⅔ cup semi-sweet chocolate chips
4 egg yolks
⅛ teaspoon salt

½ cup flaked coconut
1 teaspoon vanilla extract
4 egg whites
¼ cup sifted confectioners' sugar
½ cup heavy cream, whipped

Combine cream cheese and light cream in top part of double boiler. Beat until well blended. Add chocolate chips. Heat over hot water, stirring, until chocolate chips melt. In a bowl, beat egg yolks and salt. Fold part of chocolate mixture into egg yolks; then fold into chocolate mixture. Cook over hot water, stirring constantly, until slightly thickened. Stir in coconut and vanilla. Cool. Preheat oven to 325°. Beat egg whites until soft peaks form. Gradually add confectioners' sugar, beating until stiff peaks form. Fold chocolate mixture into beaten egg whites. Pour into an ungreased 1-quart casserole. Set in a pan of hot water. Bake 1 hour, or until a knife inserted in center comes out clean. Serve immediately topped with whipped cream.
Yield: 6 serving

COTTAGE CHEESE CUPCAKES

¼ cup butter
1¾ cups brown sugar, packed
Grated rind of 1 lemon
1 egg, beaten
1½ cups creamed cottage cheese
1½ cups unsifted all-purpose flour

½ teaspoon salt
½ teapoon baking soda
½ teaspoon ground cinnamon
¼ teaspoon ground ginger
¼ teaspoon ground nutmeg
1 cup chopped raisins

Preheat oven to 350°. Grease 18 muffin tins. In a bowl, cream butter with ¾ cups brown sugar until light and fluffy. Add lemon rind and egg. Beat thoroughly. Press cottage cheese through a sieve or strainer. Stir in cottage cheese and remaining brown sugar into butter mixture. Mix well. Combine dry ingredients; then fold into cottage cheese mixture. Stir in raisins. Fill muffin tins ⅔ full. Bake 30 to 35 minutes.
Yield: 18 cupcakes.

GEORGIA PEACH CHEESECAKE

Crust:
½ cup butter, melted
2 cups quick oats
⅔ cup brown sugar

Filling:
1 8-oz. package cream cheese,
   softened
¾ cup creamed cottage cheese

¾ cup granulated sugar
3 eggs
1 teaspoon vanilla extract

Glaze:
 1 cup orange juice
 2 teaspoons cornstarch
 ¼ cup sugar

Topping:
 2 10-oz. packages frozen sliced
   peaches, thawed and drained
Nutmeg

Crust:
Preheat oven to 350°. In a mixing bowl, combine butter and quick oats. Add brown sugar. Press mixture onto the bottom and about 1½-inches up the side of an ungreased 9-inch spring-form pan. Bake 10 minutes. Cool.

Filling:
Beat cream cheese and cottage cheese with an electric mixer set on high for 10 minutes, or until smooth. (There may be small lumps.) Slowly add sugar, keep beating. Add eggs, one at a time, beating well after each addition. Add vanilla extract. Pour into crumb crust. Bake 35-40 minutes or until firm. Cool.

Glaze:
In a saucepan, combine orange juice, cornstarch, and sugar. Bring to a boil. Boil, stirring constantly, until thick and clear. Cool. Arrange peach slices over cheesecake. Spoon glaze over peaches. Sprinkle with nutmeg. Chill before serving.
Yield: 8 to 10 servings.

LEMON CUSTARD

½ cup melba toast crumbs, rolled and sifted	¼ teaspoon salt
1 cup sugar	2 cups cottage cheese
¼ cup butter, melted	3 tablespoons all-purpose flour
2 egg yolks	½ cup milk
Juice of 1 lemon	½ cup heavy cream, whipped
Rind of 1 lemon, grated	2 egg whites
¼ teaspoon mace	⅓ cup chopped walnuts

Combine crumbs, ½ cup sugar, and butter. Sprinkle on bottom of greased baking dish. Beat egg yolks with remaining sugar. Add lemon juice and rind, mace, salt, and cottage cheese. Blend flour with milk. Add to mixture, mix thoroughly; then press through a sieve. Add whipped cream to mixture. Beat egg

whites until stiff. Fold into mixture. Mix lightly. Pour mixture into baking dish; sprinkle with walnuts. Set baking dish in pan of hot water. Bake 1 hour at 350°. Serve cold.
Yield: 8 servings.

REFRIGERATOR COOKIES

½ cup shortening	½ teaspoon salt
½ cup brown sugar	½ teaspoon cinnamon
1 egg	¼ teaspoon nutmeg
1¾ cup sifted all-purpose flour	¼ teaspoon ground cloves
½ teaspoon baking soda	⅓ cup cottage cheese, sieved

Cream shortening with sugar. Beat in egg. In a bowl, sift flour with baking soda, salt, cinnamon, nutmeg, and cloves; add sieved cottage cheese. Stir mixture together to make a stiff dough. Form into long roll; wrap in waxed paper. Chill until dough is firm enough to slice easily. Preheat oven to 375°. Cut in very thin slices. Place slices a little apart on ungreased baking sheet. Bake 10 minutes or until lightly browned.
Yield: about 35 cookies.

RHUBARB CHEESE PIE

Crust:
   1 cup graham cracker crumbs
   3 tablespoons sugar
   3 tablespoons butter, melted

Filling:

1 pound rhubarb	½ cup sugar
¾ cup sugar	2 eggs
2½ tablespoons quick-cooking tapioca	¼ teaspoon salt
1 8-oz. package cream cheese, softened	

Topping:
   1 cup dairy sour cream
   2 tablespoons sugar
   1 teaspoon vanilla extract

Crust:
Combine ingredients for crust. Press onto bottom and side of 9-inch pie pan.

Filling:
Cut rhubarb into ½-inch pieces; then combine with sugar and tapioca in a saucepan. Allow to stand until moistened; then set over low heat to further extract juice from rhubarb. Cover. Cook over moderate heat until fruit is tender and tapioca is almost clear. Cool. Beat cream cheese and sugar until fluffy. Beat in eggs, one at a time, beating only to blend. Add salt. Spoon rhubarb mixture over crumbs. Carefully spread cream cheese mixture over rhubarb. Preheat oven to 350°. Bake 30 to 35 minutes or until set. Cool.

Topping:
Increase oven temperature to 425°. Combine sour cream, sugar, and vanilla. Spread over baked filling. Bake 5 to 8 minutes to glaze. Cool.
Yield: 8 to 10 servings.

SNACK-TIME COOKIES

1 cup butter	2½ cups all-purpose flour
1 8-oz. package cream cheese, softened	1 teaspoon baking powder
¾ cup sugar	½ teaspoon salt
¾ cup brown sugar, packed	1 12-oz. package semisweet chocolate pieces
1 egg	½ cup chopped walnuts
1 teaspoon vanilla extract	

Preheat oven to 375°. Cream butter. Add cream cheese and sugar. Mix until light and fluffy. Stir in egg and vanilla. Combine flour, baking powder, and salt. Mix well with cream cheese mixture. Mix in chocolate pieces and nuts. Drop mixture by rounded teaspoonfuls about 2'' apart onto greased cookie sheet. Bake 15 to 18 minutes or until lightly browned.
Yield: about 65 cookies.

TANGY CHEESECAKE

Crust:

1 cup graham cracker crumbs	3 tablespoons sugar
2 tablespoons butter, melted	1 teaspoon nutmeg

Filling:

2 tablespoons unflavored gelatin	1 teaspoon grated lemon rind
½ cup cold water	¼ cup lemon juice
2 egg yolks	1 teaspoon vanilla extract

½ cup sugar
½ teaspoon salt
½ cup milk
2 cups cottage cheese, creamed

1 teaspoon ground ginger
1 teaspoon ground cinnamon
1 cup heavy cream, whipped
2 egg whites

Crust:
Combine ingredients for crust. Set aside ⅓ cup for topping. Press crumb mixture into an 8 x 8 x 2-inch baking pan.

Filling:
Soften gelatin in cold water; set aside. In the top portion of double boiler, combine egg yolks, sugar, and salt. Stir in milk. Cook over simmering water until mixture thickens slightly. Stir softened gelatin into hot custard, stir to dissolve completely. Cool. Cream cottage cheese thoroughly. Add cottage cheese, lemon rind and juice, vanilla, ginger, and cinnamon to cooled custard. Mix well. Fold whipped cream into mixture. Beat egg whites until stiff. Fold into mixture. Pour over crumb crust. Sprinkle with crumbs. Chill until set, about 4 hours.
Yield: 10 to 12 servings.

STRAWBERRY CHEESE TARTS

Tart shells:
1½ cup all-purpose flour
½ teaspoon salt

½ cup shortening
4 to 6 tablespoons water

Filling:
1 cup sugar
½ cup cold water
1 quart strawberries, washed
 and sliced
2 tablespoons cornstarch

2 tablespoons cold water
2 3-oz. packages cream cheese,
 softened
3 tablespoons light cream

Tart shells:
Preheat oven to 475°. Sift together flour and salt. With a pastry blender, cut in shortening. Gradually stir in just enough water to hold the mixture together. Divide pastry into 10 equal parts. Roll out. Fit into individual tart pans. Bake 8 to 10 minutes. Cool.

Filling:
Bring sugar and water to a boil; then pour over berries in a bowl. Cool. Drain. Reserve juice. In a saucepan, combine cornstarch and water. Add 1½ cups of juice. Cook 10 minutes, stirring frequently, to form a clear, thick glaze. Cool.

Combine cream cheese and light cream. Spread a layer of cream cheese mixture on bottom of baked tart shells; then arrange a layer of berries over the cheese. Pour about two tablespoons of cornstarch mixture over each tartlet, to glaze the berries. Let stand until glaze is set.
Yield: 10 tarts

BREADS

"Whose bread I eat, his song I sing"

An old German saying

BREAD WITH WHEAT GERM

½ cup wheat germ
3 cups all-purpose flour, unsifted
3 tablespoons sugar
4½ teaspoons baking powder
1 teaspoon salt

1 8-oz. package shredded Swiss cheese
2 eggs
1⅓ cups milk
¼ cup corn oil

Preheat oven to 350°. In a mixing bowl, combine wheat germ, flour, sugar, baking powder, salt, and cheese. Beat in eggs, milk, and oil. Beat until smooth. Grease a 9 x 5 x 3-inch loaf pan; pour in batter. Bake for 1 hour. Cool on rack.
Yield: 1 loaf.

CARAWAY CHEESE MUFFINS

1⅓ cups unsifted all-purpose flour
1 tablespoon double-acting baking powder
½ teaspoon salt
1 tablespoon sugar

1 cup grated sharp Cheddar cheese
1 teaspoon caraway seeds
1 egg, slightly beaten
2 tablespoons all-purpose oil
¾ cup milk

Preheat oven to 400°. Grease 12 muffin tins. In a mixing bowl, combine flour, baking powder, salt, and sugar. Mix thoroughly. Stir in cheese and caraway seeds with a fork. Combine egg, oil, and milk. Add to dry ingredients; stir only to combine. Fill muffin tins ⅔ full. Bake 25 minutes.
Yield: 12 muffins.

CHEESE BREAD

1 package compressed yeast
¼ cup warm water (about 110°)
1¼ cups hot milk
1¼ cups grated Cheddar cheese

1 tablespoon sugar
3½ cups unsifted all-purpose flour
1 teaspoon salt

Dissolve yeast in warm water. Let stand 10 minutes. Pour hot milk over cheese in a saucepan. Cook, stirring, over low heat just until cheese melts. Remove from stove, pour into mixing bowl. Add and stir in sugar and 1 cup flour. Cool to lukewarm. Add yeast mixture; beat until smooth. Cover bowl with a damp cloth. Let rise in a warm place 1 hour. Beat in remaining flour and salt. Let stand 10 minutes. Knead on a lightly floured board until smooth and elastic, adding more flour if needed to make a soft dough that handles easily. Place dough in a greased bowl, turn to grease top. Cover. Let rise in warm place until double in volume, about 45 minutes. Grease bottom of 9 x 5 x 3-inch loaf pan. Punch dough down; then pull sides into center. Shape into loaf; place in pan. Brush top with a little milk. Cover, using a damp cloth. Let rise until double in volume, about 1 hour. Preheat oven to 375°. Bake 1 hour.
Yield: 1 loaf.

CHEESE STICKS

1¾ cups unsifted flour
2 teaspoons baking powder
¾ teaspoon salt
⅓ cup shortening

1 cup grated sharp Cheddar cheese
¾ cup milk
3 tablespoons poppy seeds (optional)

Preheat oven to 450°. Combine flour, baking powder, and salt. Add shortening; cut in with a pastry blender until mixture resembles coarse cornmeal. Add cheese; stir in with a fork. Slowly pour in milk to make a soft (not sticky) dough. Lightly flour a board; knead a few times. Roll pieces of dough into sausage-like shapes about ½-inch in diameter and 4-inches long. If desired, roll in poppy seeds. Place on ungreased baking sheet. Bake 10 minutes.
Yield: 24 cheese sticks

COTTAGE CHEESE CRISPS

1 cup sifted all-purpose flour
¼ teaspoon salt
½ teaspoon baking powder
½ cup butter

1 tablespoon milk
½ cup cottage cheese
Paprika
½ teaspoon celery seed

Sift together flour, salt, and baking powder. With a pastry blender, cut in butter. Add milk to cottage cheese, then stir into flour mixture. Make small ball of dough upon floured board and roll into ⅛-inch thickness. Cut into ½-inch strips. Place strips on baking sheets and brush with milk; sprinkle with paprika and celery seed. Preheat oven to 425°. Bake 10 to 12 minutes or until lightly browned.

FILLED CHEESE ROLLS

1 cake fresh active yeast	¼ cup sugar
¼ cup lukewarm water	1 teaspoon salt
¾ cup milk	1 egg, beaten
2 tablespoons butter	3 cups sifted all-purpose flour

Filling:
 1 cup cottage cheese
½ cup peanut butter, crunch style

Soften yeast in lukewarm water. Heat milk to boiling point. Remove from heat. Add butter, sugar, and salt. Cool to lukewarm. Add yeast and egg. Stir in flour, making a soft dough. Knead until satiny; place in a bowl and cover with a damp cloth. Allow to rise until double in size, about 1 to 1½ hours. Punch dough down and let it rest 10 minutes; then roll out ¼-inch thick. Combine cottage cheese and peanut butter. Spread over dough; roll it up as for jelly roll, and cut off 1-inch slices. Place cut side down on greased baking sheet 1-inch apart. Cover. Let rise until light. Preheat oven to 400°. Bake 15 to 20 minutes.
Yield: 1 dozen cheese rolls.

NIPPY CHEESE BREAD

2 cups self-rising flour	¼ cup milk
1 tablespoon sugar	¼ cup butter, melted
1 tablespoon minced onion	2 eggs
½ teaspoon Italian herbs	2 tablespoons grated Parmesan cheese
¼ cup dry vermouth	

Preheat oven to 400°. In a mixing bowl, combine flour, sugar, onion, and herbs. Combine wine, milk, butter, and eggs. Pour all at once into flour mixture. Stir only to moisten flour. Grease and paper-line a 1½-quart round casserole dish. Sprinkle top with grated cheese. Bake 25-35 minutes or until slightly browned.
Yield: 1 loaf.

SOUR CREAM

Take the good with the bad,
the sweet with the sour.

Anonymous

SOUR CREAM

To many people, sour cream is a good topping for a baked potato and nothing more. A survey made in 1970 showed that the greatest popularity of sour cream was as a baked potato topping, as a salad dressing, or as a dip. While there is no denying that sour cream tastes good that way, it has a lot more to offer if given a chance. It can be used in a wide range of dishes from soups to desserts and makes everyday food taste extraordinary. It seems to have a gourmet quality that can transform an ordinary noodle dish into an elegant beef stroganoff with a European touch.

Sour cream as it once was made in the home was the result of cream that had been allowed to go "sour." The dairy sour cream we buy today is "cultured cream." In other words, light cream is inoculated with a commercial starter and the process is controlled to obtain a smooth, heavy-bodied uniform product.

According to one statistic, American housewives repeat their range of main dish recipes every two weeks. Perhaps cooking with sour cream will open up some new avenues in cookery.

NOW THAT YOU ASK...

Q. Is sour cream known by any other name?
A. Yes. It is also marketed as "cultured cream," "cultured sour cream," "sour market cream," and "salad cream."

Q. How is it made?
A. Cream that is 18 percent milk fat is pasteurized and homogenized. It is then cooled to 72° F. and innoculated with a culture (*Streptoccocous Lactis*). If rennet is to be added, it is done while the cream is stirred. The mixture is then allowed to ripen at 72°F. for 15 hours and then thoroughly chilled to 35°-40° F. It is gently stirred and finally packaged.

Q. What is "mock sour cream?"
A. A product that has a taste similar to sour cream but is made from different ingredients. It is used as a salad dressing or as a garnish, but not in cooking.

It may be made by combining a cup of creamed cottage cheese, a cup of buttermilk, two teaspoons of lemon juice. Mix until throughly blended.

Q. What is "sour half and half?"
A. It is sour cream made with less milk fat (10 to 12 percent).

129

Q. Can "sour half and half" be substituted for sour cream?

A. Yes, except in recipes that require the creamier texture, such as cookies and cakes.

Q. What is "non-cultured sour cream?"

A. Cream that has been made to gel by the addition of edible food acids with or without a stablizer and emulsifier. It may contain flavoring material and added non-fat milk solids.

Q. What is the calorie content of sour cream?

A. 1 tablespoon = 30 calories
   ½ cup = 240 calories

Q. What is the best way to store it?

A. In its original carton in the coldest part of the refrigerator.

Q. Can it be frozen?

A. It should not be frozen. Research, however, has shown that some sour cream-based dishes may be successfully frozen.

Q. What is the best method of measuring sour cream for a recipe?

A. Use the same measurements as you would for dry ingredients.

Q. What is the difference between sour cream and yogurt?

A. They are both cultured milk products. But sour cream is made from cream, and yogurt is made from milk or skim milk. The bacteria cultures are also different for each product.

Q. Can sour cream be whipped?

A. Yes. Whip as for whipping cream. When first whipped it will thin out, then it takes about 5 minutes to whip. It will double in volume but it won't thicken as much as whipping cream.

APPETIZERS

BANANA CREAM DIP

1 cup dairy sour cream	2 teaspoons fresh lemon juice
3 tablespoons honey	3 firm ripe bananas

Combine sour cream with honey and lemon juice. Grate peeled bananas into mixture; stir to blend thoroughly. Serve with canned or fresh pineapple wedges, melon balls, or other fruits that can be speared on cocktail "picks."
Yield: about 3 cups.

CAULIFLOWER DIP

1 medium cauliflower	Dash Worcestershire sauce
½ pound blue cheese	Salt to taste
1 cup dairy sour cream	

Carefully break cauliflower into bite-sized flowerettes, trimming as needed to remove small leaves and stems. In a small bowl, mash cheese with a fork. Add sour cream and mix well. Stir in Worcestershire sauce and salt. Place dip in the center of a serving tray and surround with flowerettes.
Yield: about 1½ cups.

DEVILED DIP

1 large Bermuda onion	1½ teaspoons prepared horseradish
2 cups dairy sour cream	1 teaspoon Worcestershire sauce
4 tablespoons sweet pickle relish	½ teaspoon salt
4 teaspoons dry mustard	

Hollow out Bermuda onion, being careful to leave the outer part intact. Combine remaining ingredients. Reserve 1 tablespoon pickle relish. Chill. When ready to serve, fill onion with mixture. Garnish with remaining relish. Serve with crackers.
Yield: about 2 cups.

DILL DIP

½ cup shredded Cheddar cheese	½ teaspoon dill weed
1 tablespoon prepared horseradish	1 cup dairy sour cream

Combine cheese, horseradish, and dill weed. Blend in sour cream. Cover. Chill 1 hour or longer before serving. Serve with wheat wafers.
Yield: 1¼ cups.

FRUIT CURRY DIP

2 cups dairy sour cream	1 teaspoon curry powder
¾ cup crushed pineapple, drained	½ teaspoon garlic salt

Combine ingredients. Refrigerate. Serve with crackers.
Yield: 3 cups.

HAM CANAPES

1 cup finely chopped cooked ham	2 tablespoons vinegar
2 teaspoons grated orange rind	¼ cup chopped onion
4 to 5 teaspoons soy sauce	½ cup chopped almonds, toasted
¼ cup dairy sour cream	

Combine ingredients. Chill. To serve, spoon on large crackers or onto flattened bread triangles spread with butter.
Yield: about 1½ cups.

HAM AND SOUR CREAM SPREAD

½ pound cooked ham	½ cup dairy sour cream
6 small dill pickles	1 tablespoon prepared mustard
6 ounces Swiss cheese	¼ teaspoon Worcestershire sauce
3 hard-cooked eggs	

In a blender, grind ham, pickles, cheese, and eggs. Blend in sour cream, mustard, and Worcestershire sauce. Use as a spread for crackers or for open-faced sandwiches.
Yield: about 3 cups.

RED ROSÉ

1 Edam cheese	1 7-oz. can tuna fish
1 cup dairy sour cream	1 teaspoon minced onion
1 cup rosé wine	

Slice 1-inch piece from top of cheese. Carefully remove cheese from shell, keeping shell intact. Grate cheese. Flake tuna fish. Combine sour cream, rosé, onion, cheese, and tuna fish. Beat with wire whisk until light and fluffy. Fill cheese shell with mixture. Serve with assorted crackers.
Yield: about 4 cups.

TUNA SPREAD

1 7-oz. can tuna, drained	1 teaspoon dry mustard
½ cup finely chopped celery	¼ teaspoon leaf thyme
3 tablespoons chopped pimiento- stuffed olives	1½ teaspoons unflavored gelatin
	1 cup dairy sour cream

Break tuna into small pieces; then combine with celery, olives, mustard and thyme. Slowly fold gelatin into sour cream; then combine with tuna mixture. Cover, refrigerate one hour or longer.
Yield: about 2 cups.

TANGY SOUR CREAM DIP

2 cups dairy sour cream
3 tablespoons prepared horseradish
2 teaspoons Worcestershire sauce
1 teaspoon celery seed

1 teaspoon salt
½ teaspoon paprika
4 teaspoons pimiento-stuffed olives, finely chopped

Combine ingredients. Chill. Serve with crackers or chips.
Yield: about 2 cups.

SALADS 'N' DRESSINGS

FROSTY MOLD

2 3-oz. package lime-flavored gelatin
2 cups boiling water
1 cup dairy sour cream

1 20-oz. can crushed pineapple, drained
⅓ cup chopped pecans
1 8-oz. package dates, diced

Combine gelatin with water; stir until gelatin is dissolved. Chill until thick, but not completely set. Whip with electric mixer or hand beater until frothy and light. Add sour cream and mix well. Fold in drained crushed pineapple, pecans, and dates. Pour into lightly greased 6-cup mold. Unmold onto serving plate.
Yield: 8 to 10 servings.

FROZEN FRUIT SALAD

1 cup dairy sour cream
2 tablespoons frozen concentrated orange juice, thawed
1 tablespoon lemon juice
1 teaspoon sugar
½ teaspoon prepared mustard

¼ teaspoon salt
1 8-oz. can crushed pineapple, drained
¾ cup halved, seeded grapes
¾ cup diced canned peaches
Salad greens

Chill bowl and beaters; then whip sour cream about 5 minutes, until thick and doubled in volume. In mixing bowl, combine orange and lemon juice, sugar, mustard, and salt. Slowly blend in sour cream. Fold in fruit. Pour into a salad mold and freeze. When ready to serve, unmold on salad greens.
Yield: 6 servings.

HONEY-ORANGE SALAD

3 large oranges, peeled
⅓ cup dairy sour cream

1 head bibb lettuce
12 pear halves

Dressing:
1 cup dairy sour cream
1½ tablespoons honey
¼ teaspoon grated lemon rind

1 tablespoon toasted sesame seed
1 tablespoon poppy seed

Cut each orange into 6 slices. For each salad spread 3 orange slices with sour cream and put together. Arrange lettuce on plates. Place orange slices between 2 pear halves; stand on lettuce with large end of pear as base. Combine sour cream, honey, and lemon rind. Top each salad with dressing. Sprinkle with sesame and poppy seeds.
Yield: 6 servings.

HOT CRAB SALAD

2 7-oz. cans flaked crab meat
¼ cup Rosé wine
½ cup dairy sour cream
½ teaspoon dry mustard
½ teaspoon salt
Dash of cayenne

¼ teaspoon dry thyme
1 cup chopped celery
2 hard-cooked eggs, chopped
½ cup slivered almonds
¼ cup grated Parmesan cheese
¼ cup butter, melted.

Preheat oven to 325°. In mixing bowl, toss crab meat gently with Rosé wine. Marinate 30 minutes. Combine sour cream, mustard, salt, cayenne, and thyme; gently toss with crab mixture. Add celery and eggs. Pour mixture into buttered 1½-quart baking dish. Sprinkle with almonds and cheese; then sprinkle with butter. Bake 25-30 minutes.
Yield: 4-6 servings.

POTATO SALAD mit SOUR CREAM

6 cups hot diced potatoes	¾ cup boiling water
⅓ cup finely chopped onion	1½ tablespoons prepared mustard
9 slices bacon, diced	1 cup dairy sour cream
3 tablespoons bacon drippings	1 tablespoon finely chopped parsley
⅓ cup vinegar	Salt and pepper to taste
1 tablespoon sugar	

Combine hot cooked potatoes and onion. Fry bacon until crisp; drain on absorbent paper. Pour off all but 3 tablespoons of bacon drippings. Add vinegar, sugar, water, and mustard to bacon drippings; stir until sugar is dissolved. Add hot mixture to potatoes and toss gently until most of the moisture is absorbed. Fold in sour cream, parsley, bacon, salt, and pepper. Blend well. Serve warm or cold.
Yield: 6 to 8 servings.

SCANDINAVIAN SALAD

½ cup toasted blanced slivered almonds	1 teaspoon Worcestershire sauce
½ cup sliced green pepper	⅑ teaspoon ground nutmeg
2 cups shredded cabbage	½ teaspoon dill weed
1 cup dairy sour cream	½ teaspoon salt
1 tablespoon wine vinegar	Lettuce
	1 5-oz. can sardines

Toss together almonds, green pepper, and cabbage. Combine remaining ingredients except for lettuce and sardines. Toss with cabbage mixture. Turn mixture into salad bowl lined with lettuce. Arrange sardines over top.
Yield: 4 to 6 servings.

SOUR CREAM DRESSINGS

CREOLE

1 cup dairy sour cream
½ cup bottled cocktail sauce

Combine ingredients. Serve on vegetable salads.
Yield: 1½ cups.

HORSERADISH

| 1 cup dairy sour cream | 1 teaspoon lemon juice. |
| 2 tablespoons prepared horseradish | Salt and pepper to taste |

Combine ingredients. Serve on ham, tongue, meatloaf, or hamburgers.
Yield: 1 cup.

INDIENNE

1 cup dairy sour cream
1½ teaspoons curry powder
Salt and pepper to taste

Combine ingredients. Serve on cold cuts, lamb, pineapple, and fresh or canned fruits.
Yield: 1 cup.

BASIC DRESSING

1 cup dairy sour cream	2 tablespoons sugar
¼ cup wine vinegar	Dash of cayenne pepper
1 teaspoon salt	½ teaspoon grated onion

In mixing bowl, combine ingredients. Beat until stiff.
Yield: about 1¼ cups.

A La MEXICANA

| 1 cup dairy sour cream | ½ teaspoon garlic salt |
| 1½ teaspoons chili powder | Salt and pepper to taste |

Combine ingredients. Serve with baked beans, frankfurters, cold beef, or hamburgers.
Yield: 1 cup.

CAPER

1 cup dairy sour cream
2 tablespoons crushed capers
Salt and pepper to taste

Combine ingredients. Serve with fish.
Yield: 1 cup.

DILL DRESSING

½ cup dairy sour cream
1 tablespoon dried dill
1 teaspoon lime juice

⅓ cup milk
½ cup mayonnaise

Combine ingredients. Serve on seafood or vegetable salads.
Yield: about 1 cup.

CARAWAY DRESSING

1 cup dairy sour cream
2 tablespoons white vinegar
1 tablespoon sugar

½ teaspoon salt
1 teaspoon caraway seed

Combine ingredients. Serve with tossed green salads.
Yield: about 1 cup.

SWEDISH HERRING SALAD

1 cup diced pickled herring
1 cup diced cooked potatoes
1 cup diced pickled beets, drained
  (reserve juice)
1 cup chopped apple
3 tablespoons chopped pickles

2 cups dairy sour cream
2 tablespoons beet juice
1 teaspoon prepared mustard
1 teaspoon sugar
½ teaspoon salt
1 egg, hard-cooked, for garnish

Combine herring, potatoes, beets, apple, and pickles. Blend sour cream with beet juice, mustard, sugar, and salt; fold into herring mixture. Rinse a 4-cup mold with cold water; then pack mixture into mold. Chill. Sieve egg yolk and white separately. When ready to serve, unmold and garnish with alternating rows of sieved yolk and white of egg.
Yield: 4 to 6 servings.

FRUIT SALAD DRESSING

2 eggs	**⅓ cup lemon juice**
½ cup sugar	**1 teaspoon grated orange rind**
1 cup orange juice	**2 cups dairy sour cream**

In saucepan slightly beat eggs. Mix in sugar, orange juice. Place over low heat; cook, stirring constantly, until mixture thickens. Remove from heat. Blend in lemon juice and orange rind. Pour into serving bowl. Cool; then slowly fold in sour cream. Cover. Refrigerate until ready to serve. Serve over fruit salad.
Yield: about 3 cups.

ROQUEFORT DRESSING

1 cup dairy sour cream	**1 tablespoon wine vinegar**
¼ cup Roquefort cheese, crumbled	**½ teaspoon salt**
1 tablespoon sugar	**Dash of pepper**

Combine dairy sour cream and cheese. Add remaining ingredients. Chill. Serve with tomato slices, fish fillets, or as a dip.
Yield: 1¼ cups.

SOUPS

ASPARAGUS CREAM SOUP

2 10-oz. packages frozen, cut-up asparagus	**2 tablespoons butter**
1¾ cups water	**2 tablespoons all-purpose flour**
1 cup dairy sour cream	**1 teaspoon salt**
1 chicken bouillon cube	**Dash of pepper**
¼ cup boiling water	**3 cups milk**

Place asparagus and water in a saucepan. Cover. Bring to a boil; then lower heat. Simmer until tender. Pour asparagus and liquid into a blender. Puree. Place in mixing bowl. Blend sour cream into asparagus. Set aside. Dissolve bouillon cube in boiling water. In a large saucepan, melt butter. Blend in flour, salt, chicken bouillon, and pepper. Remove from heat. Slowly pour in milk. Place over medium heat; cook, stirring constantly, until thickened. Cook 2 more minutes. Stir in asparagus mixture. Heat.
Yield: 8 cups.

AUGUST SOUP

2 cups finely chopped cucumber
1 cup chopped cooked carrots
4 cups dairy sour cream
1½ cups milk
1 clove minced garlic

1 teaspoon salt
⅛ teaspoon pepper
2 teaspoons chopped chives
2 teaspoons chopped parsley

Combine cucumber, carrots, and sour cream. Add milk. Mix garlic with salt, pepper, chives, and parsely. Add to sour cream mixture. Chill 4 to 6 hours. Serve in chilled bowls or cups.
Yield: 6 to 8 servings.

BORSCH

1 pound soup bone with meat (beef, pork or spareribs)
8 cups water
1 teaspoon salt
⅓ cup dry lima beans
1 medium onion
4 medium beets
1 medium potato, diced
1½ cups shredded cabbage
¾ cup diced string beans

1 cup chopped beet greens (optional)
1 8-oz. can tomato sauce with mushrooms
1 beef bouillon cube
Juice of one lemon
Salt and pepper to taste
1 tablespoon chopped fresh dill (optional)
1 cup dairy sour cream

Cover soup bone with cold water. Add salt and slowly bring to a boil. Skim off foam as it accumulates. Reduce heat to simmer. Add lima beans. Shred the onion on the coarse grate. Add to soup pot. Cover and simmer about 1 hour. Cut beets into very thin strips; then add to pot with remaining vegetables. Stir in tomato sauce, lemon juice, and bouillon cube. Partially cover with the lid. Allow to simmer about 1 hour or until the vegetables are tender. Season with salt and

pepper. Add dill. Remove meat. Set aside. (If desired, meat may be removed from bone and added to the borsch.) Pour out 1 cup of soup to cool. Combine cooled soup with sour cream. Slowly stir into borsch. Do not reheat after sour cream has been added. Soup can be made ahead and reheated the next day. If it is, do not add sour cream until ready to serve.
Yield: 8 to 10 generous servings.

COLD BLUEBERRY SOUP

1 12-oz. package frozen
  blueberries, thawed
2 cups water
½ cup honey

1 stick cinnamon
1 thinly sliced lemon
2 cups sour cream
½ cup red wine

In a saucepan, combine blueberries, water, honey, cinnamon, and sliced lemon. Bring to boil. Reduce heat and simmer, uncovered, 15 minutes. Strain. Do not force pulp through sieve. Discard pulp. Chill. Beat in sour cream and wine.
Yield: 4 cups.

CURRY VICHYSSOISE

10 to 12 leeks
¼ cup butter
1 10½-oz. can condensed cream of
  chicken soup, undiluted
4 cups boiled and diced potatoes
1 cup heavy cream
2 teaspoons salt

¼ teaspoon white pepper
1 teaspoon curry powder
1 cup heavy cream
2 cups dairy sour cream
1 cup half and half
Chopped chives

Slice white part of leeks very thin. In a saucepan melt butter; sauté leeks. Add soup. Simmer 20 minutes. Add potatoes and cream. Simmer 10 more minutes. Sieve mixture. Add salt, white pepper, curry powder, and cream. Chill overnight. When ready to serve, add sour cream and half and half. Serve in chilled soup bowls. Garnish with chopped chives.
Yield: 8 servings.

HEARTY BEEF SOUP

¼ cup butter
1 cup water

1 3-oz. package smoked sliced beef,
  cut into small pieces.

2 cups shredded potatoes
2 tablespoons chopped onion
1 tablespoon all-purpose flour
4 cups milk

1 8¾-oz. can whole kernel corn
¼ teaspoon celery seed
1 cup dairy sour cream
Salt and pepper to taste

Melt butter in a saucepan. Add water, potatoes, and onion. Cover. Bring to a boil. Lower to simmer; cook 20 minutes or until potatoes are tender. Stir in flour. Cook 1 minute. Slowly pour in milk, stirring constantly. Stir in cut beef. Pour in corn and liquid. Add celery seed. Gradually blend in sour cream. Salt and pepper to taste.
Yield: 8 to 10 servings.

PLUM SOUP

1 30-oz. can purple plums, pitted
2 tablespoons fresh lemon juice
⅛ teaspoon salt

Dash of ground cinnamon
1½ cups dairy sour cream

Drain plums; then push pulp through sieve. Combine pulp with lemon juice and enough water to make 4 cups. Add salt and cinnamon. Beat in sour cream. Chill.
Yield: 4 servings.

MAIN DISHES-MEATLESS DISHES

BOMBAY CHICKEN

¾ cup all-purpose flour
1 teaspoon salt
¼ teaspoon pepper
1 teaspoon ginger
6 whole chicken breasts, split
Butter for frying

1 chicken bouillon cube
3 tablespoons all-purpose flour
1½ cups milk
1 cup dairy sour cream
Additional ginger, salt, and pepper

Combine flour, salt, pepper, and ginger in plastic bag; shake well. Drop in chicken pieces 2 at a time; shake until chicken is well coated. Melt butter in large skillet. Add chicken and brown slowly on all sides, adding more butter as needed. As pieces brown, remove to baking dish. Bake, uncovered 30 to 35 minutes at 350° or until chicken is tender. In the meantime, add butter to drippings in skillet to make approximately 3 tablespoons combined butter and drippings. Mash in bouillon cube. Stir in 3 tablespoons flour; heat until bubbly. Slowly stir in milk;

cook, stirring constantly, until thickened. Remove from heat; stir in sour cream. Season with ginger, salt, and pepper to taste. Pour mixture over chicken. Bake an additional 10 minutes, uncovered.
Yield: 6 to 8 servings.

CHICKEN PACIFIC

2 cups dairy sour cream
1 teaspoon tarragon
1 teaspoon thyme
½ teaspoon garlic powder
1 teaspoon paprika
2½ teaspoons salt
6 chicken breasts
1½ cups cornflake crumbs
¼ cup butter
1 cup cooked, cleaned small shrimp
¼ cup diced olives

Preheat oven to 350°. In mixing bowl, combine 1 cup sour cream with spices. Wash chicken breasts and wipe dry. Dip pieces into sour cream mixture, then into cornflake crumbs; coating well. Melt butter in baking dish; then place chicken, skin side down, in dish and bake 45 minutes. Pour remaining sour cream into saucepan, add shrimp and olives. Heat over low flame. Just before serving pour sauce over baked chicken.
Yield: 6 servings.

CHICKEN WITH MUSHROOMS

½ pound fresh mushrooms
½ cup butter
3 tablespoons chopped pimiento
¼ cup all-purpose flour
2 cups chicken broth
½ cup milk
1 tablespoon Worcestershire sauce
½ teaspoon salt
2 egg yolks, beaten
½ cup dairy sour cream
2 cups diced cooked chicken
1 7-oz. package frozen snow peas, thawed

Gently wash mushrooms; then pat dry and slice. In a large saucepan melt butter; add mushrooms and sauté 2 minutes. Stir in pimiento and flour. Slowly blend in broth, milk, Worcestershire sauce, and salt. Cook, stirring, over low heat until mixture thickens and comes to a boil. Mix egg yolks with sour cream; stir into thickened sauce. Add chicken and snow peas. Heat gently; do not boil. Serve with hot rice.
Yield: 6 servings.

HOT TURKEY SALAD

½ cup chopped celery
¼ cup sweet pickle relish
¼ cup almonds, slivered
½ cup teaspoon salt
¼ cup chopped pimiento

1 cup dairy sour cream
½ cup mayonnaise
2 cups chopped cooked turkey
6 pieces of toast

In saucepan, combine all ingredients except toast. Cook over very low heat. Serve hot, over slices of toast.
Yield: 6 servings.

STUFFED SQUASH ON THE HALF SHELL

3 medium acorn squash
Salt
¼ cup butter
2 cups dairy sour cream
1 7½-oz. can diced crab meat

1½ cups cooked, diced turkey
  or chicken
1 tablespoon wine vinegar
½ cup shredded Swiss cheese

Preheat oven to 350°. Wash squash. Cut in half lengthwise and remove seeds and fibers. Place cut side down on baking sheet; bake 35-40 minutes. Turn cut side up, sprinkle with salt and dot with butter. Bake an additional 15-20 minutes, or until squash is tender. In saucepan, combine sour cream, crab meat, turkey, and wine vinegar. Simmer just to serving temperature. Place squash halves on serving dish, fill with sour cream mixture, sprinkle with Swiss cheese and serve at once.
Yield: 6 servings.

BEEF ROLLS

2 pounds ground beef
2 eggs
2 teaspoons salt
¼ teaspoon pepper
1 tablespoon finely chopped onion
1 3-oz. jar pimiento-stuffed olives
Flour

3 tablespoons butter
½ cup milk
2 cups dairy sour cream
¼ pound Cheddar cheese, grated
½ teaspoon salt
Dash Tabasco sauce
⅓ cup sliced stuffed olives

Preheat oven to 400°. Mix together beef, eggs, salt, pepper, and onion. Form into 12 oblong rolls; poke a whole olive into center of each roll. Coat with flour. In large skillet melt butter. Set skillet over moderate heat and brown rolls well on all

sides, add more butter if needed. Place beef rolls in baking dish. Add milk to drippings in skillet; place over low heat and stir constantly 1 minute. Remove from heat. Slowly stir in sour cream, cheese, salt, Tabasco sauce, and sliced olives. Pour mixture over beef rolls. Bake 10 to 12 minutes.
Yield: 6 to 8 servings.

MEATBALLS BAKED IN SOUR CREAM

2 pounds ground beef
½ cup finely chopped onion
⅓ cup chopped pimiento-stuffed
 olives
2 eggs, slightly beaten
1 teaspoon salt
¼ teaspoon pepper
¼ cup butter

2 tablespoons all-purpose flour
½ cup water
1 teaspoon lemon juice
½ teaspoon Worcestershire sauce
¼ teaspoon paprika
¼ teaspoon salt
1 cup dairy sour cream

Combine beef, onion, olives, eggs, salt, and pepper; mix until just blended. Shape into medium-sized balls. In skillet melt butter; slowly brown meatballs on all sides. Transfer meatballs into a shallow baking dish. Pour fat from skillet except 2 tablespoons; blend in flour. Add remaining ingredients except sour cream; cook over medium heat, stirring constantly, until mixture thickens. Cook 2 more minutes. Preheat oven to 350°. Remove skillet from heat. Slowly blend in sour cream. Pour gravy over meatballs. Place baking dish in oven for 10-15 minutes.
Yield: 8 servings.

OLD FAVORITE STROGANOFF STEW

2½ pounds lean boneless stewing beef
3 tablespoons oil
½ pound sliced fresh mushrooms
3 tablespoons all-purpose flour
2½ cups boiling water
¼ cup finely chopped onion
¼ teaspoon garlic salt

1 beef bouillon cube
2 tablespoons Worcestershire sauce
1 teaspoon salt
1 cup dairy sour cream
2 tablespoons tomato paste
2 tablespoons chopped fresh parsley

Cut meat into 2-inch pieces. Heat oil in a large skillet; then brown meat well on all sides, about 15 minutes. Remove; set aside. Add mushrooms and sauté 5 minutes.

Stir in flour; cook, stirring, 2 minutes. Slowly pour in water. Add onion, garlic salt, bouillon cube, 1 tablespoon Worcestershire sauce, salt, and meat. Cover skillet, lower heat. Simmer 1½ hours or until meat is tender. Combine sour cream, tomato paste and remaining Worcestershire sauce; stir into meat. Heat, but do not boil. Stir in parsley. Serve over hot noodles.
Yield: 6 servings.

POT ROAST

1 tablespoon butter
4 pound beef pot roast
1 teaspoon salt
¼ teaspoon pepper
½ teaspoon monosodium glutamate

1 10½-oz. can condensed cream of celery soup
½ cup onion rings
1 cup dairy sour cream
1 teaspoon prepared horseradish

Gravy:
2 cups drippings
¼ cup water
2 tablespoons all-purpose flour

Melt butter in a large skillet; then brown meat slowly on both sides. Transfer to baking dish. Sprinkle with salt, pepper, and monosodium glutamate. Spoon soup over roast. Add onions; cover. Bake 2½ to 3 hours at 325° or until meat is tender. Pour 2 cups of drippings into saucepan; set aside. Blend horseradish into sour cream; then spread over meat.
Yield: 6 to 8 servings.

Gravy:
Heat drippings in saucepan until it reaches a boil; remove from heat. Slowly stir water into flour; then add to drippings, stirring constantly. Return to heat, cook, stirring, until thick. Cook two minutes longer.

SPANISH STEAK WITH SOUR CREAM SAUCE

3 pounds round steak, about ¾-inch thick
2 teaspoons salt
⅛ teaspoon pepper
½ cup all-purpose flour
2 tablespoons butter

1 1-pound can tomatoes
1 small green pepper, chopped
⅓ cup chopped onion
1 tablespoon all-purpose flour
1 cup dairy sour cream

Cut meat into 6 serving pieces. Season with salt and pepper; cover meat with flour and score with sharp knife. Cover both sides again with flour. In large skillet melt butter over low heat. Place meat in skillet; slowly brown on both sides. In mixing bowl, combine tomatoes, green pepper, and onion. Pour over meat. Cover skillet and simmer 2 to 2½ hours or until meat is tender. Place meat on a serving plate and keep warm. Blend 1 tablespoon flour with the liquid in skillet. Cook, stirring constantly, until thickened (about 5 minutes). Remove from heat. Slowly stir sour cream into skillet. Pour gravy over meat and serve.
Yield: 6 servings.

HUNGARIAN VEAL WITH POPPY SEED NOODLES

2 pounds veal	1 teaspoon salt
2 tablespoons shortening	¼ teaspoon garlic salt
¼ cup chopped onion	⅓ teaspoon pepper
1 3-oz. can sliced mushrooms and liquid	2 cups dairy sour cream
	1 6-oz. package noodles
1 tablespoon all-purpose flour	3 tablespoons butter
2 teaspoons paprika	1 tablespoon poppy seeds

Preheat oven to 300°. Cut veal into 1-inch cubes. In skillet, brown meat in shortening. Remove from skillet, place in baking dish. In skillet add onion and drained mushrooms. Brown lightly. Slowly blend in flour. Stir in mushroom liquid, paprika, salt, garlic salt, and pepper. Cook until thickened. Remove from heat. Slowly add sour cream. Pour over meat. Cover and bake 1 hour. While meat is in oven, prepare noodles according to package directions. Drain. Add butter and poppy seeds and toss lightly. Serve veal cubes over poppy seed noodles.
Yield: 4 servings.

PAPRIKA SCHNITZEL

6 veal cutlets	½ cup chopped onion
3 tablespoons all-purpose flour	2 tablespoons all-purpose flour
2 teaspoons paprika	1 cup milk
1 teaspoon salt	1 bay leaf, crushed
2 tablespoons butter	½ teaspoon caraway seed
1 4-oz. can sliced mushrooms and liquid	1 cup dairy sour cream
	Salt to taste
1 tablespoon butter	

Combine flour, paprika, and salt; coat meat. In a large skillet melt butter. Over very low heat; brown veal, 10 minutes each side. Drain mushroom liquid into skillet with veal; cover and simmer until meat is very tender. Place meat on serving dish; keep warm. Add butter, onion and mushrooms to the drippings in skillet. Sauté until onion is tender. Stir in flour. Remove skillet from heat; slowly add and stir in milk. Add bay leaf and caraway seed. Cook over medium heat. Stir constantly, until gravy thickens. Cook for 2 more minutes. Slowly blend in sour cream. Season to taste. Pour sauce over veal and serve immediately. *Yield: 6 servings.*

VEAL STEW

2 pounds veal stew meat, cut up	2 tablespoons paprika
½ cup all-purpose flour	1 4-oz. can sliced mushrooms,
2 teaspoons salt	drained
½ teaspoon pepper	¼ cup water
¼ cup salad oil	1 cup dairy sour cream
1 large onion, sliced	½ cup toasted blanched slivered
1½ cups white wine	almonds

Coat veal in a combination of ¼ cup flour, 1 teaspoon salt, and pepper. In a large skillet brown veal in oil over medium heat. Add onion, wine, paprika, mushrooms, and remaining salt. Cover skillet. Simmer 1 hour. Combine flour and water; stir into stew liquid and cook, stirring, until thickened. Stir in sour cream and almonds, mixing well. Serve over noodles or rice. *Yield: 4 to 6 servings.*

MUSHROOMS IN SOUR CREAM

8 slices bacon	1 teaspoon Worcestershire sauce
1 pound fresh mushrooms	1 cup dairy sour cream
½ cup finely chopped onion	4 slices toasted bread
1 teaspoon all-purpose flour	

Fry bacon until crispy. Drain on paper towels. Reserve 2 tablespoons bacon fat. Pour off the rest. Wash and slice mushrooms (to keep them from turning in color, sprinkle with a little lemon juice and toss lightly). Over low heat, sauté mushrooms and onion in skillet for 10 minutes. Add and stir in flour. Add Worcestershire sauce and sour cream. Simmer, stirring constantly, until mixture is heated through. Spoon mixture over toast. Garnish with bacon pieces. *Yield: 4 servings.*

ORANGE GINGER PORK CHOPS

6 pork chops
¼ cup orange juice
1 large orange

½ teaspoon salt
1 teaspoon ground ginger
¾ cup dairy sour cream

In skillet, brown chops well on both sides. Pour in orange juice, cover skillet and simmer 30 minutes. Peel and slice orange. Season chops with salt and ginger; then top each with orange slice. Cover skillet; cook 15 more minutes or until chops are tender. Place chops in baking dish and top each with sour cream. Broil about 1 minute. Serve immediately.
Yield: 6 servings.

HAWAIIAN HALIBUT

2 Halibut steaks, about 2 pounds
2 teaspoons prepared mustard
2 tablespoons brown sugar
1 cup crushed pineapple
¼ cup soft bread crumbs

1¼ cups dairy sour cream
2 tablespoons pineapple syrup
¾ teaspoon salt
½ teaspoon ground ginger

Preheat oven to 350°. Place 1 steak in shallow baking dish. Spread with 1 teaspoon mustard and sprinkle with 1 tablespoon brown sugar. Spread ½ cup pineapple over steak. Cover with 2 tablespoons bread crumbs. Combine sour cream, pineapple syrup, salt, and ginger. Pour ½ of the mixture over fish. Place the second steak over the first and repeat the procedure. Bake 30 minutes.
Yield: 6 servings.

SEAFOOD CASHEW CASSEROLE

1 6-oz. package frozen crab meat
1 9-oz. package frozen lobster tails
¼ cup butter
1 cup chopped celery
¼ cup chopped onion
¼ cup chopped green pepper
½ cup water

2 tablespoons milk
2 tablespoons cornstarch
1 tablespoon soy sauce
3 drops Tabasco sauce
1 cup dairy sour cream
1 3-oz. can chow mein noodles
⅓ cup coarsely chopped cashew nuts

Thaw and drain crab meat; cut into pieces. Cook lobster following directions on package. Remove meat from shells and cut into pieces. Melt butter in skillet. Sauté celery, onion, and green pepper in butter until tender. In bowl, combine

water, milk, cornstarch, soy and Tabasco sauces. Add and stir into skillet. Simmer, stirring constantly, until mixture thickens, about 5 minutes. Remove from heat. Stir in sour cream; then add lobster, and crab meat. Preheat oven to 350°. Butter 1½-quart baking dish. Pour in mixture. Sprinkle noodles and nuts over top. Bake 30-40 minutes.
Yield: 4 servings.

SHRIMP BAKED WITH SOUR CREAM

1 1-pound package frozen shrimp
1 cup dairy sour cream
¼ cup butter, softened
1 tablespoon all-purpose flour
1 tablespoon sugar
¼ teaspoon dry mustard
¼ teaspoon basil
⅛ teaspoon salt
2 tablespoons lemon juice
⅓ cup dry bread crumbs
¼ cup butter, melted

Cook shrimp as directed on package; drain. Place shrimp in a baking dish or divide into 4 individual ramekins. Heat sour cream in saucepan over low heat until warm. Add softened butter; heat until melted, stirring constantly. Remove from heat. Preheat oven to 375°. In mixing bowl combine flour, sugar, dry mustard, basil, and salt. Blend flour mixture into sour cream. Stir in lemon juice. Place over low heat and cook, stirring constantly, until thickened. Spoon mixture over shrimp. Combine crumbs and ¼ cup melted butter; then sprinkle over sauce. Bake 10-12 minutes. Serve piping hot.
Yield: 4 servings.

SHRIMP SUCCESS

2 tablespoons butter
1 4-oz. can sliced mushrooms
1 pound shrimp, cooked and cleaned
1 teaspoon salt
1 teaspoon Worcestershire sauce
1 tablespoon all-purpose flour
1 cup dairy sour cream

In large skillet, melt butter. Add mushrooms and shrimp; cook over medium heat until heated through. In bowl, combine flour, salt, Worcestershire sauce, and sour cream. Stir into shrimp mixture. Cook over low heat, stirring constantly, until sauce begins to bubble. Serve over rice or toast.
Yield: 4 servings.

SHRIMP WITH ALMONDS

2 tablespoons chopped onion
1 tablespoon chopped green pepper
1 tablespoon butter, melted
¼ teaspoon curry powder
1 10½-oz. can condensed cream of
  mushroom soup

¼ cup milk
2 cups cooked shrimp
⅓ cup dairy sour cream
⅓ cup toasted blanched slivered
  almonds

Sauté onion and pepper in melted butter until soft. Add curry powder, soup, and milk; mix well. Heat thoroughly. Mix in shrimp and sour cream. Heat; do not boil. Stir in almonds. Serve over hot rice.
Yield: 4 servings.

GOLDEN POTATOES MAGNIFIQUE

6 medium potatoes, boiled
1 medium onion, grated
1 teaspoon salt
2 3-oz. packages pimiento cream
  cheese, softened

2 cups dairy sour cream
2 cups grated sharp Cheddar cheese

Preheat oven to 350°. Peel and slice potatoes; then place in buttered baking dish. Sprinkle grated onion over potatoes and season with salt. Blend softened cream cheese with sour cream. Spoon mixture over potatoes. Sprinkle with cheese. Bake, uncovered, 30-35 minutes.
Yield: 4 to 6 servings.

PILAFF WITH SOUR CREAM

3 cups chicken broth
1½ cups uncooked rice
¾ teaspoon salt
1 clove garlic, crushed
⅓ cup chopped parsley

¼ cup chopped green onions
2 tablespoons anchovy paste
3 tablespoons tarragon wine vinegar
Dash of pepper
1½ cups dairy sour cream

In large saucepan, combine broth, rice, and salt. Bring to boil; stir once. Cover, lower heat, and simmer until liquid is absorbed, about 15 minutes. In bowl combine remaining ingredients with sour cream. Serve over hot rice.
Yield: 6 to 8 servings.

RICE ROMANOFF

3 cups cooked rice
¼ cup finely chopped green onions
1½ cups large curd cottage cheese
1 clove garlic, minced
1 cup dairy sour cream

¼ cup milk
¼ teaspoon hot pepper sauce
½ teaspoon salt
½ cup grated Parmesan cheese

Preheat oven to 350°. In large bowl, combine rice and onions. Add and blend in remaining ingredients except Parmesan cheese. Butter 1½-quart baking dish. Pour mixture into casserole. Sprinkle with Parmesan cheese. Bake 25 minutes. *Yield: 6 servings.*

SUMMERTIME SUPPER DISH

⅔ cup milk
2 cups biscuit mix
2 tablespoons melted butter
4 tomatoes
Salt and pepper to taste

1 cup dairy sour cream
¾ cup mayonnaise
1 cup grated sharp Cheddar cheese
½ cup finely chopped onion
Paprika

Preheat oven to 425°. In mixing bowl combine milk and biscuit mix. Stir to a soft dough; then beat vigorously until stiff. Place on floured surface and knead 8 to 10 times. Roll out thinly to fit into a 13 x 9 x 2-inch baking dish. If necessary, stretch dough to fit, pushing dough up sides to make a slight rim. Brush dough with melted butter. Cut tomatoes into slices; arrange over dough and season with salt and pepper. In mixing bowl combine sour cream, mayonnaise, cheese, and onion; spoon over tomatoes, spreading mixture to barely reach edge of dough. Sprinkle with paprika. Bake 10 minutes at 425°; lower heat to 350°, bake 10 to 15 minutes longer.
Yield: 4 to 6 servings.

WARM SOUR CREAM SAUCE FOR COOKED VEGETABLES

2 tablespoons butter
2 tablespoons minced onion
2 teaspoons sugar
1 teaspoon wine vinegar

⅛ teaspoon pepper
1½ cups dairy sour cream
¼ cup chopped walnuts

Melt butter on top of double boiler. Add onion and sauté until tender. Stir in sugar, vinegar, and pepper. Slowly blend in sour cream. Place top of double

boiler over warm, not boiling water. Heat over low heat until sauce is warm. Serve over cooked vegetables.
Yield: 6 servings.

BREADS

CINNAMON COFFEECAKE

½ cup butter
1 cup sugar
2 eggs
1 teaspoon vanilla extract
¼ teaspoon lemon juice

2 cups all-purpose flour
1 teaspoon baking powder
1 teaspoon baking soda
1 cup dairy sour cream

Brown sugar mixture:
¼ cup firmly packed light
   brown sugar
¼ cup chopped walnuts

1 tablespoon sugar
1½ teaspoons cinnamon

Preheat oven to 350°. In a large mixing bowl, cream butter. Slowly add sugar. Beat until light and fluffy. Beat in eggs, one at a time. Fold in vanilla extract and lemon juice. Sift together flour, baking powder, and baking soda. Add dry ingredients to creamed mixture alternately with sour cream, beginning and ending with dry ingredients. Pour half the batter into a greased 10-inch tube pan. Combine ingredients for brown sugar mixture. Sprinkle batter with mixture. Pour in remaining batter. Bake 45-50 minutes. Cool on wire rack 10 minutes before turning out of pan. Serve warm.
Yield: about 8 servings.

CINNAMON NUT BREAD

¼ cup butter
1½ cups firmly packed light
   brown sugar
2 eggs
2½ cups sifted all-purpose flour
1½ teaspoons cinnamon

1½ teaspoons baking soda
¾ teaspoon baking powder
½ teaspoon salt
1½ cups dairy sour cream
1½ cups chopped walnuts

Cream butter in large bowl. Slowly add brown sugar. Beat until light and fluffy. Beat in eggs, one at a time. Sift together flour, cinnamon, baking soda, baking

powder, and salt. Add dry ingredients to creamed mixture alternately with sour cream, beginning and ending with dry ingredients. Stir in nuts. Pour mixture into a greased 9 x 5 x 3-inch loaf pan. Bake 45-50 minutes. Remove from pan. Cool on wire rack.
Yield: 1 loaf.

FLAKY BISCUITS

2 cups sifted all-purpose flour	¼ cup butter
1 tablespoon baking powder	¾ cup dairy sour cream
½ teaspoon salt	¼ cup milk
¼ teaspoon baking soda	Butter, melted

Preheat oven to 450°. Sift together flour, baking powder, salt, and baking soda. With pastry blender, cut in butter until mixture resembles coarse meal. Blend in sour cream. Slowly add milk; stir until dough sticks together. Knead batter on lightly floured board. Roll out about ½ inch thick. Cut out with a floured 2-inch biscuit cutter. Place on ungreased baking sheet. Bake 10-12 minutes. Remove from oven: brush tops with melted butter. Serve warm.
Yield: 16 to 18 biscuits.

FRUIT KUCHEN

2 cups sifted all-purpose flour	¼ cup butter, melted
½ cup sugar	1½ cups thinly sliced fresh peaches
4 teaspoons baking powder	(or fresh fruit in season such
¾ teaspoons salt	as apples, pears, or plums)
¼ teaspoon mace	2 tablespoons sugar
1 egg	1 teaspoon cinnamon
1 cup milk	1 cup diary sour cream

Preheat oven to 350°. Sift together flour, sugar, baking powder, salt, and mace. Beat together egg and milk; add to dry ingredients. Stir in melted butter; combine just till blended. Spread batter in a greased 12 x 7½ x 2-inch baking dish. Place fruit slices in rows on batter. Combine sugar and cinnamon; sprinkle over fruit. Bake 35 minutes. Spread sour cream over kuchen. Return to oven 5 more minutes to glaze. Place on wire rack 10 minutes to cool. Cut into serving pieces; serve warm.
Yield: 10 to 12 servings.

GOLDEN COFFEECAKE

1 package active dry yeast
¼ cup warm water
¾ cup dairy sour cream
1 egg, slightly beaten
2 tablespoons butter, melted

3 cups sifted all-purpose flour
6 tablespoons sugar
1 teaspoon salt
⅛ teaspoon baking soda
Melted butter

Topping:
¾ cup dairy sour cream
¾ cup firmly packed light
  brown sugar

½ teaspoon vanilla extract
¼ cup chopped walnuts

In a mixing bowl dissolve yeast in water. Blend in sour cream, beaten egg, and butter. Sift together dry ingredients; slowly stir into yeast mixture. Knead batter on floured surface 5 minutes or until smooth. Place in buttered bowl; brush with melted butter. Set in warm place until doubled. Form roll about 25 inches long; place in buttered ring mold, 6½ cup. Again set in warm place to double. Preheat oven to 350°. Bake 30 minutes. Turn out on rack to cool.

Topping:
In a saucepan combine sour cream and sugar. Place over medium heat, cook, stirring occasionally, until mixture makes a soft ball in cold water or reaches 225° on candy thermometer. Add vanilla extract. Cool mixture to lukewarm. Beat until it starts to thicken. Spoon over coffeecake; drizzle with walnuts.

PRUNE BREAD

¼ cup butter
1 cup sugar
3 eggs
2⅓ cup all-purpose flour
  1 teaspoon ground allspice
  1 teaspoon ground cinnamon
  1 teaspoon baking powder

½ teaspoon baking soda
½ teaspoon salt
½ teaspoon ground cloves
½ cup dairy sour cream
1 tablespoon lemon juice
1 cup cooked, pitted chopped prunes

Preheat oven to 350°. In a mixing bowl cream butter. Slowing add sugar, beating until light and fluffy. Beat in eggs, one at a time. Sift together dry ingredients. Add dry ingredients to mixture alternately with sour cream, beginning and ending with dry ingredients; combine just until blended. Combine lemon juice with prunes; mix into batter. Pour batter into a greased 9 x 5 x 3-inch loaf pan. Bake 50-60 minutes. Remove from pan. Cool on rack.
Yield: 1 loaf.

SOUR CREAM BISCUITS

2 cups all-purpose flour	1 teaspoon salt
1 tablespoon baking powder	1 cup dairy sour cream
¼ teaspoon baking soda	¼ cup milk

Preheat oven to 450°. In a mixing bowl, sift together flour, baking powder, baking soda, and salt. Blend in sour cream. Stir in milk to make a soft dough. Knead gently on lightly floured board. Roll ½-inch thick; then cut with biscuit cutter. Place on baking sheet. Bake 10 minutes. Serve hot.
Yield: 12 biscuits.

SOUR CREAM PANCAKES

4 eggs, separated	¾ teaspoon baking soda
1 cup dairy sour cream	½ teaspoon salt
1 cup small curd cottage cheese	1 tablespoon sugar
¾ cup sifted all-purpose flour	butter

Beat egg yolks until creamy. Combine sour cream and cottage cheese; add to egg yolks and blend thoroughly. Sift flour with baking soda and salt; add to cottage cheese mixture. Beat egg whites until stiff gradually adding sugar; then gently fold into mixture. Lightly butter a heated griddle or frying pan. Drop batter by spoonfuls onto griddle; cook until bubbly, turn, brown on other side.
Yield: about 20 pancakes.

DESSERTS

APPLE DANDY

6 tart apples	¼ cup granulated sugar
¼ cup brown sugar	½ teaspoon salt
½ teaspoon cinnamon	1 cup dairy sour cream
2 tablespoons butter	3 tablespoons light cream
¼ cup all-purpose flour	

Preheat oven to 325°. Slice apples; place in a well-buttered 1-quart casserole. Combine brown sugar and cinnamon; cut in butter. Sprinkle over apples. Combine remaining ingredients. Spread over apples. Bake 45-50 minutes. Serve warm.
Yield: 6 servings.

CHOCOLATE FUDGE

2 cups sugar	¼ teaspoon salt
1 cup confectioners' sugar	1 tablespoon butter
1 cup dairy sour cream	1 teaspoon vanilla extract
3 squares unsweetened chocolate	1 cup chopped walnuts

In large heavy saucepan, combine sugars, sour cream, chocolate, and salt. Bring mixture to boil, stirring occasionally. Cook over low heat until mixture reaches 234° on candy thermometer. Do not stir. (Mixture should form soft ball when dropped in cold water.) Stir in butter and vanilla extract. Cool to lukewarm. Add nuts. Beat until mixture becomes thick and loses its shine. Butter 8-inch square pan. Pour in mixture. When firm, cut in squares.
Yield: 1½ pounds.

FROZEN STRAWBERRY PIE

Crust:
1½ cups vanilla wafer crumbs
½ cup finely chopped walnuts
½ cup butter, melted

Filling:

1 10-oz. package frozen strawberries, thawed but not drained	1 egg white
½ cup sugar	1 cup dairy sour cream

Preheat oven to 350°. Combine crust ingredients; blend thoroughly. Press firmly and evenly on botton and sides of a 10-inch pie pan. Bake 8-10 minutes. Cool.

Filling:
In a large bowl combine strawberries, sugar, and egg white. Using electric mixer, beat at high speed for 10 minutes or until soft peaks form. Carefully fold sour cream into mixture. Spoon into crust. Place in freezer. When thoroughly chilled, make swirls on top.
Yield: about 8 servings.

GLAZED CAKE

3 3-oz. squares unsweetened chocolate	3 eggs
	2 teaspoons vanilla extract

½ cup water
1 cup dairy sour cream
½ cup butter
1 cup sugar
½ cup firmly packed
light brown sugar

2 cups sifted cake flour
1½ teaspoons baking powder
1 teaspoon baking soda
1 teaspoon salt

Filling and Frosting:
2 tablespoons butter, softened
3½ to 4 cups confectioners' sugar

6 tablespoons dairy sour cream
1 teaspoon vanilla extract

Chocolate Glaze:
1 cup semisweet chocolate pieces
2 tablespoons milk
½ cup dairy sour cream

Preheat oven to 350°. Grease 2 round 9-inch cake pans; dust with flour. Combine chocolate and water in a saucepan; place over low heat until chocolate melts, stirring constantly. Cool. Blend in sour cream. Set aside. In mixing bowl, cream butter. Combine sugars; then slowly add to creamed butter, beating until fluffy. Beat in eggs, one at a time. Add vanilla extract. Sift together dry ingredients; then add to creamed mixture alternately with sour cream mixture, beginning and ending with dry ingredients. Pour batter evenly into pans. Bake 30-35 minutes. Cool in pans on racks 5 minutes; then turn onto racks and cool. Frost and fill with sour cream filling and frosting and chocolate glaze.
Yield: about 10 servings.

Filling and Frosting:
In a mixing bowl, cream butter. Slowly blend in sugar. Add sour cream and vanilla extract; stir until smooth. (A little milk can be added to make frosting spread evenly.) Spread frosting thinly between layers and top and sides of cake.

Chocolate Glaze:
In a saucepan combine chocolate pieces with milk; set oven low heat until chocolate melts. Stir constantly. Remove from heat; stir in sour cream. Cool. Glaze over sour cream frosting.

GOLDEN CREAM PIE

1 9-inch baked pie shell
1½ cups dried apricots

¼ cup sugar
¼ teaspoon almond extract

½ cup light corn syrup
2 eggs
2 cups dairy sour cream

½ teaspoon vanilla extract
2 tablespoons toasted, slivered
   almonds

Preheat oven to 325°. Cook apricots following package directions. Drain. Stir cooked apricots into corn syrup. Pour into pie shell. Beat eggs well. Combine eggs, sour cream, sugar, and extracts; pour over apricots. Bake until cream is set, about 10 minutes. Garnish with slivered almonds. Cool. Chill 2½ hours or until cream is set.
Yield: About 8 servings.

HONEY CAKE

1 cup honey
½ cup butter
1 cup brown sugar
4 eggs, separated
3 cups all-purpose flour
2 teaspoon baking soda

½ teaspoon baking powder
1 teaspoon cinnamon
¼ teaspoon salt
1 cup dairy sour cream
1 cup chopped walnuts

Preheat oven to 325°. Bring honey to a boil; then cool. Cream butter with sugar. Add egg yolks; beat until light and fluffy. Beat in honey. Sift flour and dry ingredients; then add to honey mixture alternately with sour cream. Stir in nuts. Beat egg whites until stiff. Fold into the batter. Grease a 10-inch tube cake pan; then pour in mixture. Bake 50-55 minutes.
Yield: about 8 servings.

JUST PEACHY

2 cups all-purpose flour
¾ teaspoon salt
4 teaspoons baking powder
¼ teaspoon mace
½ cup sugar
1 cup milk

1 egg, well beaten
¼ cup butter, melted
1½ cups fresh peaches, sliced
1 teaspoon cinnamon
2 tablespoons sugar
1 cup dairy sour cream

Preheat oven to 375°. Sift together first five dry ingredients. Combine milk, egg, and butter. Add to dry ingredients, stir just until blended. Grease a 2-quart baking dish. Pour in batter; arrange peaches on top. Combine cinnamon and sugar; sprinkle over peaches. Bake 35 minutes. Remove from oven; cover evenly with sour cream. Return to oven and bake an additional 5 minutes.
Yield: 6 servings.

LITTLE OATMEAL CAKES

2½ cups oatmeal
 1 teaspoon salt
 3 tablespoons sugar
 ¼ cup butter, melted

1 cup dairy sour cream
 ¼ cup butter, melted
 ½ cup oatmeal

Preheat oven to 375°. Mix together first three ingredients. Blend in butter and sour cream. Wrap mixture in wax paper and chill until easy to handle. Shape into 1-inch balls and place on baking sheets. Dip bottom of drinking glass in melted butter, then in oatmeal. Use to flatten balls of dough. Bake 20-25 minutes.
Yield: 4 dozen.

NINA'S SUPER FROSTED COOKIES

½ cup butter, softened
1½ cups firmly packed light
    brown sugar
 2 eggs
 1 teaspoon vanilla extract
 1 cup dairy sour cream
2½ cups all-purpose flour
 1 teaspoon baking soda

½ teaspoon salt
½ teaspoon baking powder
¼ teaspoon ground nutmeg
¼ teaspoon ground cinnamon
¼ teaspoon ground ginger
½ cup finely chopped walnuts
¾ cup raisins

Cream Frosting:
 ¼ cup butter
 2 cups confectioners' sugar
 3 tablespoons dairy sour cream

In a mixing bowl, cream butter and sugar. Blend well. Add eggs, one at a time, beating after each addition. Blend in vanilla extract and sour cream. Sift together flour, baking soda, salt, baking powder, and spices. Combine with creamed mixture. Add nuts and raisins. Chill until firm. Preheat oven to 400°. Drop batter from teaspoons onto greased cookie sheets about 2-inches apart. Remove from cookie sheets and frost.
Yield: 5 dozen.

Cream Frosting:
Melt butter in a saucepan over low heat, stirring constantly, until lightly browned and bubbly. Place confectioners' sugar in mixing bowl, pour browned butter over sugar. Add sour cream. Beat until smooth and creamy.

NUTTY COFFEECAKE

½ cup butter
1 cup sugar
2 eggs
2 cups cake flour, sifted
1 teaspoon baking soda
1 teaspoon baking powder

1 teaspoon salt
1 cup dairy sour cream
1 teaspoon vanilla extract
1 teaspoon lemon juice
1 8-oz. package dates, diced

Filling:
½ cup sugar
1 cup chopped pecans
1 teaspoon cinnamon

Preheat oven to 350°. Cream butter and sugar. Add eggs one at a time, beating after each addition. Sift together flour, baking soda, baking powder, and salt. Add dry ingredients alternately with sour cream. Add vanilla extract and lemon juice; blend. Fold in dates.

Filling:
Combine filling ingredients. Grease a 13 x 9 x 2-inch pan. Pour in half the batter. Sprinkle half the filling evenly over batter. Cover with remaining batter and sprinkle top evenly with remaining filling. Bake 40-45 minutes, or until top is golden.

PINEAPPLE REFRIGERATOR CAKE

½ cup butter
1½ cups confectioners' sugar
2 egg yolks
½ teaspoon lemon extract
⅓ cup finely chopped candied
   red cherries

1 cup crushed pineapple, drained
2 egg whites
1 cup dairy sour cream
18 lady fingers, split

Sauce:
1 cup dairy sour cream
2 tablespoons confectioners' sugar

2 tablespoons orange juice
¼ teaspoon grated orange rind

In mixing bowl, cream together butter and confectioners' sugar until light and fluffy. Add egg yolks, one at a time, beating well after each addition. Add lemon extract. Mix in cherries and pineapple. Beat egg whites until stiff peaks form; fold

into fruit mixture. Fold in sour cream. Line a 9 x 7 x 3-inch loaf pan with lady fingers; cover with ⅓ of mixture. Add another layer of lady fingers. Repeat, top with cream mixture. Chill overnight. Serve with cream sauce.
Yield: 8 servings.

Cream Sauce:
Combine ingredients. Refrigerate until ready to serve.

RAISIN PIE

Crust:

1 cup sifted all-purpose flour	2 tablespoons lard
¼ teaspoon salt	3 tablespoons milk
3 tablespoons butter	

Filling:

3 eggs	1 cup cooked pitted chopped prunes
¾ cup honey	1 cup raisins
1 cup dairy sour cream	½ cup chopped walnuts
1 tablespoon lemon juice	

In mixing bowl sift together flour and salt. With pastry blender, cut in butter and lard until mixture resembles small peas. Sprinkle milk over the mixture, 1 tablespoon at a time.; mixing lightly with fork after each addition. Roll into a ball. Flour flat surface, roll dough in ⅛-inch thick circle 1-inch larger than diameter of pie plate. Place in pie plate and flute edge.

Filling:
In mixing bowl beat eggs lightly. Add and blend in honey, sour cream, and lemon juice. Fold in prunes and raisins. Pour into pie shell. Sprinkle nuts over top. Bake 50-60 minutes, or until knife inserted near center comes out clean.
Yield: about 8 servings.

RASPBERRY FILLED CAKE

½ cup butter	2 cups sifted cake flour
1 cup sugar	1 tablespoon baking powder
2 eggs	½ teaspoon salt
1 teaspoon vanilla extract	⅔ cup milk

Filling:
- 1 10-oz. package frozen raspberries, thawed
- ½ cup rasberry syrup
- 2 tablespoons sugar
- 1½ tablespoons cornstarch
- 1 tablespoon lemon juice
- 1½ cups dairy sour cream

Preheat oven to 350°. In mixing bowl cream butter. Add sugar gradually and beat until light. Beat in eggs, one at a time. Add vanilla extract. Sift together cake flour, baking powder, and salt. Add dry ingredients to creamed mixture alternately with milk, starting and ending with dry ingredients. Grease two round 9-inch cake pans; dust with flour. Pour batter evenly into pans. Bake 25-30 minutes. Remove from oven; after 5 minutes turn out onto racks to cool. As cake is baking, drain raspberries; reserve ½ cup syrup. In a saucepan combine sugar and cornstarch; slowly pour in syrup. Place over medium heat, cook, stirring constantly, until thickened. Cook 2 more minutes. Add lemon juice. Chill. In mixing bowl, fold syrup and raspberries into sour cream. Use half of filling between layers of cake and the rest to cover top. Refrigerate until ready to serve.
Yield: about 10 servings.

SOUR CREAM CARAMEL FROSTING

- 1 cup brown sugar, firmly packed
- 1⅔ cups granulated sugar
- ⅔ cup dairy sour cream
- 2 tablespoons butter, softened
- 1 teaspoon vanilla extract
- Dash of salt

In saucepan, combine sugars and sour cream. Cook over low heat, stirring until blended. Bring to boil. Boil about 8 minutes over medium heat. When mixture reaches 232° on candy thermometer, remove from heat. Cool to 110°, about 40 minutes. Add remaining ingredients. Beat with a wooden spoon 10 to 12 minutes or until frosting loses its shine and is of spreading consistency. Quickly cover the top and sides of a 8-inch two-layer cake. Bowl of frosting can be placed in pan of hot water, to maintain its proper consistency, until ready to use.
Yield: about 2 cups.

SOUR CREAM SUNSHINE CAKE

- ½ cup butter
- 1 cup sugar
- 2 eggs
- 1 cup dairy sour cream
- 1 teaspoon baking soda
- 1 cup chopped dates
- 2 small oranges, peeled and chopped
- 2½ cups sifted cake flour

Topping:
  1 cup dairy sour cream
  2 tablespoons sifted confectioners'
    sugar

Preheat oven to 350°. In mixing bowl, cream butter and sugar until light and fluffy. Beat in eggs, sour cream, baking soda, dates, and oranges until well blended. Mix in flour. Grease a square 9-inch pan. Dust bottom lightly with flour. Turn batter into pan. Bake 50-60 minutes.

Topping:
Blend sour cream with confectioners' sugar. Spread topping over warm cake.
Yield: 8 to 10 servings.

STRAWBERRY RICE FLUFF PIE

  1 8-oz. package cream cheese,
    softened
  ½ cup sugar
  1 1-pound package frozen straw-
    berries, thawed and drained
  ⅓ cup juice drained from
    strawberries

  1½ tablespoons unflavored gelatin
  1 cup cold cooked rice
  1 cup heavy cream, whipped
  1 baked 9-inch pie shell

Beat cheese with sugar until light and fluffy. Add strawberries. In the top of double boiler combine gelatin and ⅓ cup juice drained from strawberries; heat over hot water until dissolved. Cool. Combine with cheese mixture. Add rice; mix well. Fold whipped cream into mixture. Turn into baked pie shell. Chill until firm.
Yield: 6 servings.

SWISS CHOCOLATE SQUARES

  1 cup water
  ½ cup butter
  1½ squares unsweetened chocolate
  2 cups all-purpose flour
  2 cups sugar

  2 eggs
  ½ cup dairy sour cream
  1 teaspoon baking soda
  ½ teaspoon salt
  ½ cup chopped walnuts

Milk Chocolate Frosting:
  ½ cup butter

  4½ cups sifted confectioners' sugar

6 tablespoons milk   **1 teaspoon vanilla extract**
1½ squares unsweetened chocolate

Preheat oven to 375°. Grease 15½ x 10½-inch jellyroll pan. In saucepan combine water, butter and chocolate; bring to a boil. Remove from heat. Combine flour and sugar; then add to chocolate. Add eggs, sour cream, baking soda, and salt. Mix well. Pour mixture into jellyroll pan. Bake 20-25 minutes. Frost; cover with nuts. Cool before cutting into squares.
Yield: about 8 squares.

Frosting:
In saucepan combine butter, milk, and chocolate. Bring to a rapid boil, stir constantly. Remove from heat. Add sugar, beating until velvety. Add and stir in vanilla.

Sir, there is no crying for shed milk,
  that which is past cannot be recall'd.

Andrew Yarranton

MILK

Milk, the oldest food to sustain man, has also undergone an evolution. It's been pasteurized, homogenized, fortified, canned, and even dried.

Nature's perfect food, as its been called, is also the most ubiquitous food product there is. Just look in the dairy case to find milk in its many guises: cheese, yogurt, butter, and sour cream, just to mention a few.

To better understand the different ways milk is prepared, below are listed the types of milk and a short description of each.

Acidophilus Milk—pasteurized skim milk to which a bacteria culture has been added. It has a tart flavor. Available only in a few areas in the United States.

Buttermilk—see page 169.

Certified Milk—originally was a means of ensuring safe milk before pasteurized milk was commonly available. Today it is produced under rigid sanitary conditions supervised by the Medical Milk Commission. Sold only in a few areas in the United States.

Chocolate Milk—whole milk flavored with a chocolate syrup or powder. Vanilla, salt, and stablizers may also be added. If made with partly skimmed milk it is usually labeled *chocolate flavored drink* or *chocolate flavored dairy drink*.

Concentrated Fresh Milk—fresh whole milk from which two-thirds of the water is removed. It is pasteurized and homogenized and has about 10.5 percent milk fat. It is reconstituted by adding water. Available only in a few areas in the United States.

Cream—milk which contains a high proportion of milk fat (also called *butterfat*).
   Half & Half contains about 12-18 percent cream.
   Heavy Cream (heavy whipping cream) contains 36 percent or more of milk fat.
   Light Cream (table cream, coffee cream) contains 18-30 percent milk fat.
   Light Whipping Cream contains 30-36 percent milk fat.

Evaporated Milk—homogenized milk from which half the water has been removed. This concentrated milk is fortified with Vitamin D, packed in cans and heat-sterilized. Cans of evaporated milk require no refrigeration until opened.

167

Filled Milk—a combination of skim milk and vegetable fat; or of nonfat dry milk, water, and vegetable fat.

Fortified Milk—milk that has been enriched with vitamins A and D, or a combination of vitamins, minerals, lactose, and nonfat dry milk. Made from whole, partially skimmed, or skim milk.

Homogenzied Milk—whole milk which has undergone a mechanical process to break up the milk fat into smaller particles. Warm milk is forced through small holes that break up the fat into particles too small to rise as cream.

Imitation Milk—a combination of several nondairy ingredients made to resemble milk. Ingredients used include vegetable fat (usually coconut oil), protein sodium caseinate or soy solids, corn syrup solids, flavoring agents, stabilizers, emulsifiers, and water.

Low-Sodium Milk—Available as a canned or fresh product for persons with restricted low-sodium diets. Fresh whole milk is passed through an ion-exchange resin to replace the sodium in milk with an equal amount of potassium. Part of the calcium and B-vitamins are lost in this process. The milk is also pasteurized and homogenized.

Nonfat Dry Milk—whole milk from which water and fat have been removed. The process involves spraying concentrated skim milk into a filtered hot-air chamber causing the remaining water to evaporate. When reconstituted it has the same food value as fresh skim milk.

Pasteurized Milk—a heating process used to destroy harmful bacteria that may be present in milk. Milk is heated to 145°F. and held for at least 30 minutes, or heated to 161°F. and held for at least 15 seconds, and then immediately cooled to 45°F. or lower.

Raw Milk—milk that has not been pasteurized.

Skim Milk—whole milk that has had the fat removed. The milk fat remaining usually varies from 1 to 2 percent. The calorie content averages 90 calories for 8 ounces.

Sweetened Condensed Milk—a mixture of whole milk and sugar from which half of the water has been removed. Sugar accounts for 40 to 45 percent of the total weight.

Two Percent Milk—whole milk and skim milk with a fat content of 2 percent. It is pasturized and homogenized and may also be fortified. The calorie content averages 150 calories for an 8 ounce glass.

Buttermilk was the name given to the liquid remaining in the churn after the butter had been removed. It was a special treat, the equivalent of licking the spoon after making icing.

Today's product is specifically made as buttermilk, under controlled laboratory conditions. A lactic acid-producing culture is added to milk and allowed to clabber. The resulting liquid is called "cultured buttermilk." Most of the cultured buttermilk made in the United States is made from skim or partly skimmed milk but whole milk or reconstituted nonfat dry milk may be used. Sometimes flecks of butter are added to give more flavor and "eye" appeal. Salt is usually added to help bring out the natural flavor.

Buttermilk should be kept covered and in the coldest part of the refrigerator until ready to be used.

Freezing buttermilk is possible but it causes the liquids and solids to separate. When thawed, stir gently to recombine the ingredients.

Following is a recipe for making buttermilk at home.

BASIC BUTTERMILK RECIPE

1 quart skim milk (or 1 quart
   reconstituted nonfat dry milk)
½ cup cultured buttermilk,
   homemade or commercial
½ teaspoon salt

Combine ingredients. Heat to 70°F., stirring well. Cover and let stand overnight or until clabbered. Stir until smooth. Refrigerate.

Butter is still made by churning. Law requires that butter contain not less than 80 percent milkfat. If no salt is added it is known as "unsalted butter" or "sweet butter."

Today butter is made from pasteurized sweet cream, or sweet cream to which a culture has been added. Cultured butter has a mildly acid flavor and aroma.

Whipped butter, usually unsalted, is made by whipping air or inert gas into butter. This process makes the butter easier to spread.

Butter should be kept refrigerated and covered so as not to absorb flavors from other foods. It may be frozen in its original container, or over-wrapped with aluminum foil or freezer paper if one plans to freeze it for several months.

Following is a recipe for making butter at home.

BASIC BUTTER RECIPE

 2 cups heavy cream
 ¼ teaspoon salt
 8 to 10 drops yellow food coloring (optional)

In a mixing bowl, beat cream at medium speed 8 to 10 minutes or until light yellow in color. The liquid should separate out. Drain off liquid; then rinse butter with cold water. Drain again thoroughly. Add salt and food coloring. Stir with fork to combine. Drain any excess liquid.
Yield: 1 cup.

NOW THAT YOU ASK...

Q Why is milk homogenized?
A. In order that the cream does not separate from the liquid.

Q. Does pasteurization of milk change its flavor or food value?
A. No.

Q. What is "cultured milk?"
A. Milk to which a cultured bacteria has been added. Examples of cultured milk are yogurt, sour cream, and buttermilk.

Q. What is fortified milk?
A. Milk that has been enriched by increasing the content of nutrients in milk. It can be fortified with vitamins A, D, multivitamin preparations, minerals, lactose, and nonfat dry milk.

Q. What natural vitamins does milk contain?
A. It has the highest source of calcium. It also provides protein and riboflavin (vitamin B_2). And it furnishes lesser amounts of niacin, vitamin A, and thiamin.

Q. How many calories in milk?
A. Buttermilk   1 cup   90 calories
   Chocolate Drink   1 cup   190 calories
   Chocolate Milk   1 cup   215 calories
   Skim Milk   1 cup   90 calories
   Whole Milk   1 cup   160 calories

Q. What effect does light have on milk?
A. Too much light destroys the riboflavin in milk and may also cause an off-flavor.

Q. What happens when milk is cooked at too high a temperature?
A. The protein in milk starts to coagulate into a surface film or a coating on the sides of the pan. In addition, off-flavors develop and the milk scorches.

Q. Can milk be frozen?

A. Yes. It may be frozen up to a month, although the flavor and appearance may alter slightly.

Q. How should dry milk be stored?

A. In a cool, dry place. After opening package be sure to reseal tightly because air causes it to become lumpy.

Q. What can one do with milk besides drink it and cook with it?

A. House plants can be shined with skim milk. Dampen a cloth with the milk; then carefully wipe each leaf.

Q. What is the word for milk in other languages?

A. Danish - maelk

Dutch - melk

French - lait

German - milch

Greek - gála

Hungarian - tej or fejni

Italian - latte

Irish - bainne

Lithuanian - pienas

Polish - mleko

Portuguese - leite

Rumanian - lapte

Russian - moloko

Spanish - leche

Swedish - mjolk

Serbo-Croatian - mleko or mlijeko

Swahili - mazina

SOUPS

AFTER SKI SOUP

1 10-oz. package frozen chopped spinach

1 cup finely chopped oysters

2 cups milk

1½ cups cream

1 teaspoon salt

¼ teaspoon garlic salt

2 tablespoons butter

½ cup heavy cream

¼ teaspoon salt

Paprika

Cook spinach according to package directions. Drain. Simmer oysters in milk about 5 minutes. Add spinach, cream, salt, garlic salt, and butter. Heat to simmering point. Whip cream with salt until stiff. Pour soup into individual oven-proof bowls. Top each with whipped cream and sprinkle with paprika. Preheat broiler. Place servings under broiler to brown cream slightly. Serve immediately.

Yield: 4 to 6 servings.

ALMONDY SOUP

2 cups blanched whole almonds
2 tablespoons instant minced onion
3 cups chicken broth
5 chicken bouillon cubes

¼ teaspoon salt
½ teaspoon coriander seed
1½ cups milk
Grated orange rind

Grind almonds in a blender. In a pot, combine ground almonds, onion, chicken broth, bouillon cubes, salt, and coriander. Simmer 30 minutes. Remove from heat. Strain. Gradually stir in milk. Simmer until thoroughly heated. Serve hot or cold garnished with grated orange rind.
Yield: 4 to 6 servings.

BEAN CHOWDER

¾ cup dry beans
1½ teaspoons salt
3 cups water
1 cup diced potato
1 medium onion, chopped

¾ cup cooked tomatoes
1½ teaspoons all-purpose flour
⅓ cup finely chopped green pepper
2 tablespoons butter
1½ cups milk

In a large pot, soak beans in salted water. Boil gently, 1½ hours. Add potato and onion; cook 30 minutes. Add more water if necessary. Mix a small amount of tomato with the flour; then put remaining ingredients, except for milk, into the pot. Cook 10 minutes. Stir occasionally. Slowly stir in milk. Reheat quickly.
Yield: 4 servings.

CAPE MAY CHOWDER

10 to 12 small white onions, halved
¼ cup butter, melted
1 quart boiling water
4 to 5 medium potatoes, peeled
and thinly sliced
2 carrots, peeled and sliced
2 tablespoons Worcestershire sauce

2½ teaspoons salt
¼ teaspoon crumbled tarragon leaves
1 bay leaf
2 pounds flounder fillets, cut
into 2-inch pieces
2 cups milk
1 cup heavy cream

In a large skillet sauté onions in melted butter until golden. Cover and simmer 10 minutes. Add water, potatoes, carrots, Worcestershire sauce, salt, tarragon, and bay leaf. Bring to boiling point. Cover. Reduce heat. Simmer 10 minutes. Lay

fish on top. Cover and simmer 15 to 20 minutes longer or until vegetables are tender and fish flakes easily. Scald milk; stir in cream. Gradually pour into fish mixture. Heat only until hot. Do not boil.
Yield: 10 to 12 servings.

MAIN DISHES-MEATLESS DISHES

CHICKEN PIE

1 frying chicken, cut up	¼ cup all-purpose flour
2 cups water	1 cup light cream
½ cup chopped celery	¼ teaspoon pepper
1 tablespoon minced onion	¼ teaspoon dill weed
1½ teaspoons salt	¼ teaspoon dry mustard
1 4-oz. can mushrooms, drained	2 tablespoons dry sherry
¼ cup butter	1 unbaked pastry shell

In a pot slowly cook chicken with water, celery, onion, salt, and liquid from mushrooms for 30 minutes, or until tender. Cool chicken. Remove skin and bones, leaving meat in large pieces. Save stock. Melt butter. Stir in flour, cream, 1 cup chicken stock, pepper, dill weed, and dry mustard. Cook, stirring, until mixture boils and thickens. Stir in chicken, mushrooms, and sherry. Turn into shallow 1-quart baking dish. Top with pastry; flute and prick. Bake 25 to 30 minutes at 400° or until golden brown.
Yield: 4 servings.

CREAMED TURKEY

4 tablespoons butter	2 tablespoons dry white wine
5 tablespoons all-purpose flour	2 cups diced cooked turkey
1¼ teaspoons salt	1 cup cooked peas
2 cups milk	⅓ cup diced roasted almonds

Melt butter. Stir in flour and salt. Slowly add milk. Cook, stirring, until mixture boils and thickens. Stir in wine. Add turkey and peas. Heat thoroughly. Stir in some of the almonds. Transfer to serving dish and sprinkle with remaining almonds.
Yield: 4 servings.

SCALLOPED CHICKEN

1 cup uncooked regular rice	2 cups milk
2 chicken bouillon cubes	1½ cups Cheddar cheese, grated
3 tablespoons butter	2 tablespoons chopped pimiento
1 tablespoon chopped onion	2 cups chopped, cooked chicken
3 tablespoons all-purpose flour	½ cup grated Cheddar cheese
1 teaspoon salt	3 slices white bread, crusts
⅛ teaspoon pepper	removed and cubed
teaspoon leaf marjoram	2 tablespoons butter, melted

Preheat oven to 375°. Grease 2-quart casserole. Cook rice according to package directions, dissolving bouillon cubes in boiling water before adding rice. In 3-quart saucepan melt butter; sauté onion; stir in flour, salt, pepper and marjoram. Remove from heat, gradually stir in milk. Return to heat and cook, stirring constantly, until mixture thickens. Cook 2 additional minutes. Add 1½ cups cheese and pimiento; stir until cheese melts. Add chicken and rice; turn into casserole. Sprinkle with remaining ½ cup cheese. Toss bread cubes in butter; arrange around edge of casserole. Bake 20 minutes.
Yield: 6 servings.

SMOTHERED CHICKEN

1 chicken, cut into serving pieces	⅛ teaspoon Tabasco sauce
⅔ cup evaporated milk	¾ cup cornflake crumbs
6 teaspoons Worcestershire sauce	¼ cup sesame seed
1 teaspoon salt	2 tablespoons butter
1 teaspoon garlic salt	

Place chicken in a bowl. Combine evaporated milk, 5 teaspoons of Worcestershire sauce, salt, garlic, and Tabasco. Mix well. Pour over chicken. Cover bowl. Marinate 2 hours or longer. Combine crumbs with sesame seeds. Roll chicken in crumb mixture, coating well. Arrange chicken in shallow baking dish, skin side up. Melt butter. Stir in remaining Worcestershire sauce. Sprinkle over chicken. Preheat oven to 350°. Bake 1 hour or until tender.
Yield: 4 servings.

BEEF BOURGOGNE*

1 pound round steak, cut in cubes	1 teaspoon beef stock base
½ teaspoon garlic salt	¼ teaspoon dried thyme

1 cup chopped onion
1 cup water
1 tablespoon Worcestershire sauce

½ pound fresh mushrooms, sliced
1 cup instant nonfat dry milk
¼ cup water

Sprinkle garlic salt over beef cubes. Preheat broiler. Broil on both sides. Place meat, onion, water, Worcestershire sauce, stock base, and thyme in a skillet. Cover. Simmer 30 minutes or until meat is tender. Wash and slice mushrooms; add to skillet. Cook 10 minutes longer. Combine dry milk and water. Slowly stir into meat. Simmer until well heated.
Yield: 6 servings.

*A low-calorie dish: approximately 325 calories per serving.

CABBAGE-LAYER MEAT LOAF

8 large cabbage leaves chopped,
  cooked, and drained
½ cup instant nonfat dry milk
½ cup water
1 teaspoon salt

¼ teaspoon pepper
1 cup soft bread crumbs
1 pound ground meat
½ cup shredded cheese

Sauce:
½ cup tomato juice
1 teaspoon chili powder
2 teaspoons celery seed
½ cup catsup

1 tablespoon Worcestershire sauce
2 tablespoons vinegar
¼ cup chopped onion
1 tablespoon brown sugar

Preheat oven to 325°. Mix sauce ingredients and set aside. Cut cabbage coarsely; cook 5 minutes in boiling salted water; drain. In mixing bowl, place instant nonfat dry milk, water, salt, pepper, and crumbs; blend well with fork. Mix in meat. Pat half of meat mixture in 8-inch baking dish; cover with cabbage; add another meat layer. Heat sauce and pour over all. Sprinkle with cheese. Bake 1 hour. Remove from oven and let stand a few minutes for juices to absorb. Cut in squares to serve.
Yield: 6 to 8 servings.

CORN AND BOLOGNA CASSEROLE

6 slices bologna
2 tablespoons butter, melted
1 tablespoon minced onion

⅛ teaspoon pepper
2 teaspoons sugar
¼ cup chopped pimiento

3 eggs, slightly beaten
2 cups frozen whole kernel corn
1 teaspoon salt

1 cup instant dry milk
2 cups warm water

Preheat oven to 350°. In frying pan, brown bologna lightly in melted butter; remove from pan, set aside and keep warm. Sauté onion until tender in same pan. Mix together remaining ingredients; add cooked onion. Turn into 1½-quart casserole; place in pan of hot water. Bake 40-45 minutes, or until brown and tests done in center. Arrange crisp bologna on top.
Yield: 6 to 8 servings.

MEATBALLS OVER LIMA BEANS

2 10-oz. packages frozen lima beans
1 pound ground beef
½ cup milk
1 egg, slightly beaten
½ cup quick rolled oats, uncooked
1 medium onion, finely chopped
1 teaspoon salt
⅛ teaspoon pepper

Oil for frying
¼ cup butter
¼ cup all-purpose flour
2 tablespoons sugar
1½ teaspoons dry mustard
1 teaspoon salt
⅛ teaspoon pepper
2 cups buttermilk

Separate lima beans; then place them in bottom of a large baking dish. Combine beef, milk, egg, rolled oats, onion, salt, and pepper. Roll into 2-inch balls. Brown in hot oil in a skillet. Drain meatballs on absorbant paper; then place on top of lima beans. In a saucepan, melt butter over low heat. Blend in flour, sugar, dry mustard, salt, and pepper. Slowly add buttermilk, stirring constantly. Cook over low heat until sauce is smooth and thickened. Pour over lima beans and meatballs. Bake 1 hour at 325°.
Yield: 6 servings.

VEAL PAPRIKA NOODLE BAKE

2 pounds veal shoulder, cut in
  1-inch squares
⅓ cup all-purpose flour
1½ teaspoon salt
⅛ teaspoon pepper
¼ cup butter, melted
1½ teaspoons paprika
1 cup finely chopped onion
1 4-oz. can sliced mushrooms,
  drained

2 cups buttermilk
1 8-oz. package medium noodles
¾ cup coarsely chopped blanched
  almonds
¼ cup butter
2 teaspoons poppy seeds
Salt to taste

Preheat oven to 325°. Shake meat in paper bag with flour, salt, and pepper until well-coated. Sauté floured meat in butter until well-browned. Place meat in a 2-quart casserole; sprinkle with paprika. Sauté onion in remaining butter until golden brown. Stir in mushrooms and buttermilk; blend thoroughly. Pour sauce over meat. Bake 1 to 1½ hours or until meat is tender. Cook noodles according to package directions. Drain. Sauté almonds in ¼ cup butter until golden brown; then add poppy seeds and salt to taste; stir until well blended. To serve, spoon meat and sauce over noodles.
Yield: 6 to 8 servings.

TUNA-RICE PIE

2 cups hot cooked rice	1 7-oz. can tuna fish, flaked
1½ tablespoons butter	3 tablespoons finely chopped onion
3 eggs	¼ teaspoon salt
3 tablespoons stuffed olives, chopped fine	Dash of pepper
	Dash of nutmeg (optional)
¾ cup scalded milk	1 cup grated Swiss cheese

In a mixing bowl, combine rice and butter. Slightly beat 1 egg; then stir into rice mixture. Add olives. Spread mixture evenly over bottom and sides of a greased 9-inch pie pan to make a shell. Slightly beat remaining eggs. Gradually stir in milk; then add tuna fish, onions, and seasonings. Pour into rice-lined pan. Sprinkle with cheese. Bake 15 minutes at 400°. Reduce heat to 350° and bake 15 minutes longer.
Yield: 4-6 servings.

SEASIDE CASSEROLE

3 tablespoons butter	½ teaspoon prepared mustard
1 tablespoon chopped onion	¼ teaspoon Worcestershire sauce
¾ cup thinly sliced celery	1 6½-oz. can crab meat, flaked
3 tablespoons flour	2 hard cooked eggs, diced
1⅓ cups milk	3 tablespoons fresh chopped parsley
¾ teaspoon salt	3 tablespoons diced pimiento
⅛ teaspoon pepper	⅓ cup blanched slivered almonds
Dash cayenne pepper	

Melt butter. Add onion and celery; cover and cook 5 minutes over moderate heat. Stir in flour. Slowly add milk and seasonings. Cook, stirring, until thickened. Add crab, eggs, parsley, and pimiento. Mix. Heat thoroughly. Stir in almonds and serve at once.
Yield: 4 servings.

SHRIMP STUFFED PEPPERS*

4 whole green peppers
½ cup chopped onion
½ cup chopped celery
1 pound can whole tomatoes, drained
    and chopped
1 8-oz. can tomato juice
1 tablespoon Worcestershire sauce
1 teaspoon salt

½ teaspoon chili powder
¼ teaspoon garlic powder
½ cup instant nonfat dry milk
¼ teaspoon baking soda
1 10-oz. package frozen shelled
    shrimp
½ cup chopped green pepper

Wash, core, and remove seeds from green peppers. Set aside. In a saucepan cook onion and celery in a small amount of water until tender. Drain. Stir in tomatoes, tomato juice, Worcestershire sauce, salt, chili, and garlic powder. Combine dry milk and baking soda; then stir into mixture. Add shrimp and ½ cup chopped green pepper. Cover saucepan. Cook five minutes, or until shrimp turns pink. Spoon mixture into pepper shells; then place in baking dish. Pour remaining liquid around peppers. Cover baking dish. Bake 30 minutes at 350°.
Yield: 4 servings.

*A low-calorie dish: approximately 175 calories per serving.

YORK'S FISH FILLETS

½ cup finely chopped celery
1 small onion, finely chopped
3 tablespoons butter
1 4½-oz. can medium shrimp
1½ cups soft bread crumbs
1 egg, lightly beaten
4 teaspoons Worcestershire sauce

2½ lbs. fillets of flounder
1 10-oz. can frozen condensed
    cream of shrimp soup, thawed
½ cup milk
1 tablespoon chopped fresh parsley
⅛ teaspoon salt

Sauté celery and onion in melted butter until soft. Drain and rinse shrimp. Reserve ¼ cup for sauce. Finely chop remaining shrimp. Combine chopped shrimp with sautéed celery and onion. Stir in bread crumbs, egg, and 3 teaspoons Worcestershire sauce. Mix well. Place a heaping tablespoon of stuffing on each fillet. Roll tightly. Fasten with a toothpick if necessary. Place in a 2-quart shallow baking dish. Set aside. In a saucepan combine soup, milk, parsley, and salt with ¼ cup shrimp and 1 teaspoon Worcestershire sauce. Mix well. Heat only until hot. Pour over fish rolls. Cover. Bake 45-50 minutes at 350°, or until fish flakes with a fork.
Yield: 6 servings.

ARTICHOKE HEARTS WITH SHRIMP SAUCE

1 10-oz. package frozen artichoke
   hearts
½ cup fresh mushrooms
1 tablespoon butter, melted
1 10-oz. can frozen condensed cream
   of shrimp soup

1 cup milk
1 tablespoon sherry (optional)
1 tablespoon Worcestershire sauce
1 tablespoon grated Parmesan cheese
Dash of paprika

Cook and drain artichokes; then place in a greased 1-quart baking dish. Wash mushrooms, then pat dry. Brown mushrooms in butter; stir in soup, milk, sherry, and Worcestershire sauce. Heat until soup is thawed, stirring often. Pour over artichokes. Top with cheese and paprika. Bake 20 minutes at 375°.
Yield: 4 servings.

ARTICHOKE EGG SCRAMBLE

3 small artichokes
2 tablespoons butter
2 tablespoons chopped onion

6 eggs
½ teaspoon salt
⅓ cup milk

Wash artichokes, trim stems and pull off tough outer leaves. Cut 1-inch off top of each artichoke; then cut into thin lengthwise slices. Melt butter in a saucepan; add artichokes. Cover. Cook slowly, stirring until tender. About 15 minutes. Add onion. Beat eggs with salt and milk. Pour over artichokes. Cook slowly until set, stirring from bottom as mixture cooks.
Yield: 4 servings.

BAKED SOUFFLE

2 cups milk
2 cups soft bread crumbs
1 teaspoon salt
½ teaspoon dry mustard

Dash cayenne (optional)
2 cups grated Swiss cheese
4 eggs, separated

Preheat oven to 350°. Scald milk; add bread crumbs, salt, mustard, cayenne and cheese. Cool slightly. Beat in egg yolks. Stiffly beat egg whites; then fold into mixture. Turn into 1½-quart casserole. Bake 50 minutes or until firm yet puffy.
Yield: 4 servings.

FONDUE MONTEREY

12 slices white bread	2 cups grated Monterey Jack cheese
Soft butter	4 eggs
1 12-oz. can whole kernel corn, drained	3 cups milk
	1 teaspoon salt
1 7-oz. can green chilies, seeded and cut into strips	

Trim crust from bread. Butter one side; then cut in half. Butter a shallow baking dish. Arrange half the bread slices on the bottom; then cover with half the corn and half the chili strips. Sprinkle with grated cheese. Repeat process until all ingredients are used. Beat eggs slightly; combine with milk and salt. Pour over casserole. Cover. Refrigerate 4 or more hours. Bake 45-50 minutes at 350°.
Yield: 6 to 8 servings.

NOODLES WITH SPINACH

4 cups medium egg noodles	2 cups milk
1 10-oz. package frozen chopped spinach	1 cup soft bread crumbs
	2 cups grated American cheese
1 small onion, chopped	4 eggs
¼ cup butter	1½ teaspoons salt

Mustard Sauce:

¼ cup butter	1 teaspoon prepared horseradish
¼ cup all-purpose flour	1¼ teaspoon salt
1½ tablespoons prepared mustard	2 cups milk

Cook noodles and spinach according to package directions. Drain. Sauté onion in butter. Combine milk, bread crumbs, cheese, eggs, and salt. Stir in sautéd onion. Preheat oven to 350°. Butter a 2-quart ring mold; pour in mixture. Set in pan of hot water. Bake 45-60 minutes or until a knife inserted in center comes out clean. Place mold on rack to cool 5 minutes. Unmold on serving plate. Serve with mustard sauce.
Yield: 6 servings.

Mustard sauce:
Melt butter in a saucepan. Blend in flour, mustard, horseradish, and salt. Slowly stir in milk. Bring to a boil; boil 1 minute, stirring constantly.

PLANTATION CASSEROLE

3 tablespoons butter
2 tablespoons flour
1 small garlic clove, crushed
1 cup milk
½ teaspoon salt

Dash of pepper
1 teaspoon paprika
3 cups cooked rice
1 cup grated Swiss cheese

Melt butter. Stir in flour and garlic. Slowly stir in milk, salt, pepper, and paprika. Mixing until smooth. Arrange rice in a buttered baking dish. Pour sauce mixture over rice. Top with shredded Swiss cheese. Cover. Bake 30 minutes at 350°. Uncover. Bake 5 minutes longer.
Yield: 6 servings.

RICE BAKE

3 cups cooked rice
1 cup diced celery
1 tablespoon minced onion
1½ tablespoons flour

½ cup mayonnaise
2 teaspoons prepared mustard
Salt and pepper to taste
½ cup milk

Combine cooked rice, celery, and onion. Blend in flour, mayonnaise, mustard, salt, pepper, and milk; stir into rice mixture. Turn into a buttered 1½-quart casserole. Cover. Bake 30 minutes at 350°.
Yield: 6 servings.

GOLDEN SWEET POTATOES

3 large sweet potatoes
½ cup butter
½ cup milk

½ teaspoon salt
¼ cup brown sugar, packed
⅛ teaspoon pumpkin pie spice

Scrub potatoes; cut off ends. Place in baking pan. Bake 1 hour at 400°. Cut potatoes lengthwise into halves. Scoop pulp into a mixing bowl. Add half the butter, milk, and salt. Beat until light and fluffy. Fill shells with potato mixture. Return to oven. Cream together remaining butter, sugar, and pumpkin pie spice. Place a dollop on each potato half. Return to oven. Heat 5 minutes or until topping is melted.
Yield: 6 servings.

MUSHROOM SAUCE

1 cup milk	Dash of savory
3 tablespoons finely minced onion	1 2½-oz. can sliced mushrooms,
1 tablespoon finely chopped parsley	drained, reserve liquid
1 teaspoon grated lemon rind	2 tablespoons cornstarch
½ teaspoon salt	2 tablespoons sherry
Dash of pepper	

In a saucepan combine milk, onion, parsley, seasonings and mushrooms. Blend. Stir in mushroom liquid and cornstarch. Cook, stirring constantly, until thickened. Add sherry. Serve over fish.
Yield: about 1½ cups.

SWEET POTATOES IN ORANGE SHELLS

4 medium oranges	4 cups cooked and mashed sweet
¼ cup honey	potatoes
¼ cup butter, melted	Pecan halves
¾ cup instant nonfat dry milk	Melted butter
½ cup orange juice	

Cut oranges in half and hollow out. Mix honey, melted butter, dry milk, and orange juice; add to mashed sweet potatoes and blend. Spoon mixture into orange shells. Garnish with pecan halves. Brush with melted butter. Bake 25-30 minutes at 350°.
Yield: 8 servings.

DESSERTS

COCONUT SNOWBALLS

2 tablespoons cornstarch	½ cup chopped pecans
1 cup sugar	3 eggs, separated
¼ teaspoon salt	1 teaspoon brandy extract
2 cups milk	½ cup finely shredded coconut
2 cups cooked rice	

Preheat oven to 350°. In saucepan, combine cornstarch, ⅔ cup sugar, and salt. Stir in milk; cook until thickened, stirring occasionally. Remove from heat. Fold

in rice and nuts. Beat egg yolks slightly. Add small amount of hot mixture to eggs; mix thoroughly; stir into remaining mixture. Add brandy extract. Pour into 6 well-greased, 5-ounce custard cups; set cups in shallow pan. Pour hot water in pan, 1-inch deep. Bake 30 minutes, or until set. Cool slightly. Unmold and place on greased baking sheet. Beat egg whites until stiff but not dry. Gradually beat in remaining sugar and continue beating until whites stand in stiff peaks. Spread on top and sides of custards. Sprinkly lightly with coconut. Return to oven. Bake 5 minutes or until flecked with brown.
Yield: 6 servings.

CHOCOLATE CREAMCAKE AU BRANDY

1⅓ cups buttermilk	⅓ cup honey
2 eggs	⅓ cup brandy
1 package chocolate cake mix	

Frosting:
 2 cups whipping cream
 ¼ cup confectioners' sugar
 3 tablespoons brandy

Preheat oven to 350°. Grease and lightly flour two 9-inch cake pans. Beat buttermilk with eggs and cake mix at medium speed of electric mixer for 3 minutes. Bake 30-35 minutes; or until cake springs back when touched lightly in the center. Cool in pans 10 minutes. In a saucepan, warm honey over low heat. Stir in brandy. Place cakes on serving dish. Spoon warm syrup over layers. Cool thoroughly.

Frosting:
Combine cream with confectioners' sugar. Refrigerate 1 hour; then beat until just stiff. Slowly beat in brandy. Frost top and sides of cake. Refrigerate one hour before serving.
Yield: about 10 servings.

CUSTARD

⅔ cup sweetened condensed milk	½ teaspoon salt
2 cups hot water	1 teaspoon vanilla extract
3 egg, slightly beaten	Cinnamon

Preheat oven to 325°. Combine condensed milk and water; then gradually stir in

eggs, salt, and vanilla. Pour into a 1-quart shallow baking dish. Sprinkle with cinnamon. Place in shallow pan of hot water. Bake 40-50 minutes or until a knife inserted near center comes out clean. Cool.
Yield: 6 servings.

DANISH BUTTERMILK PUDDING

2 tablespoons unflavored gelatin
¼ cup cold water
¼ cup boiling water
1½ cups buttermilk

1 egg, beaten
½ cup sugar
¼ teaspoon salt
½ cup heavy cream, whipped

In a mixing bowl, soften gelatin in cold water; then add boiling water. Stir until dissolved. Combine egg, sugar, salt, and buttermilk. Stir until sugar and salt dissolve; then blend with gelatin mixture. Chill until slightly thickened. Fold in whipped cream. Pour into a 1-quart mold. Refrigerate until firm.
Yield: 4 to 6 servings.

FROSTED STRAWBERRIES (candy)

⅔ cup sweetened condensed milk
2⅔ cups flaked coconut
  1 3-oz. package strawberry
    flavored gelatin

½ cup ground blanched almonds
½ teaspoon almond extract
Red food coloring

Strawberry hulls:
1 cup sifted confectioners' sugar
2 tablespoons heavy cream
Green food coloring

In a mixing bowl, combine sweetened condensed milk, coconut, 3 tablespoons gelatin, almonds, and almond extract. Drop enough red food coloring into mixture to give it a strawberry color. Use about ½ teaspoon of mixture to form strawberry shapes. Place remaining gelatin on a flat plate; roll each "strawberry" to coat. Place on waxed paper. Chill. Place an open star tip on pastry bag, spoon in hull mixture. Pipe small amount atop each strawberry.
Yield: 1 pound.

HOMEMADE ICE CREAM

VANILLA:
⅔ cup sweetened condensed milk
½ cup water

1½ teaspoons vanilla extract
1 cup heavy cream

Combine sweetened condensed milk, water, and vanilla extract. Refrigerate. Whip cream to a soft custard-like consistency. Fold into chilled mixture; pour into ice cube tray. Freeze 1 hour, or until a firm mush forms. Turn into chilled, large-size electric mixer bowl. Break into pieces; beat until fluffy but not melted. Quickly return to ice cube tray. Cover with a aluminum foil. Freeze until firm. *Yield: about 1½ pints.*

COFFEE:

⅔ cup sweetened condensed milk
½ cup water
1½ teaspoons vanilla extract

1 cup heavy cream
2 teaspoons instant coffee,
   dry form

Proceed as for vanilla ice cream except stir instant coffee into mixture before pouring into ice cube tray to form firm mush.

PEPPERMINT CANDY:

⅔ cup sweetened condensed milk
½ cup water
1½ teaspoons vanilla extract

1 cup heavy cream
1 cup finely crushed peppermint
   stick candy

Proceed as for vanilla ice cream except add candy into mixture before pouring into ice cube tray to form firm mush.

HONEY-CUSTARD PASTRY

4 cups milk
1 cup farina or cream of rice
6 tablespoons butter, melted
1 teaspoon vanilla extract
½ teaspoon ground cinnamon

6 eggs
¾ cup sugar
12 strudel sheets*
¾ cup butter, melted

Syrup:

1 cup water
1 cup sugar
¼ cup honey

Small stick of cinnamon
1 tablespoon lemon juice

Heat milk over low heat until warm. Slowly add farina, stirring constantly, until it thickens and is smooth. Stir in butter until completely blended. Remove from heat. Add vanilla and cinnamon. Beat eggs until light. Gradually beat in sugar. Add farina mixture and stir well. Cool. Grease a 10 x 14 x 2-inch pan. Lay in 6 strudel sheets, brushing each sheet with melted butter. Spread mixture over pastry. Cover with remaining pastry, brushing each sheet with melted butter. With a sharp knife lighly cut 2-inch squares through the top layer of pastry only.

Bake 45 minutes at 350° or until golden. Cool slightly. Cut through to bottom of pastry. Pour lukewarm syrup over pastry. Best served warm.
Yield: 8 to 12 servings.

Syrup:
Combine water, sugar, honey and cinnamon stick. Boil 10 minutes. Remove from heat. Remove cinnamon stick and stir in lemon juice.

*See page 110   = filo - pastry

MIKE'S FAVORITE RICE PUDDING

½ cup water
⅓ cup rice
⅛ teaspoon salt
4 cups milk
1 cup sugar

1 tablespoon cornstarch
2 eggs
1 teaspoon vanilla extract
Cinnamon

In a small pan, bring water to a boil. Add rice and salt. Parboil 5 minutes. Heat milk over low flame until lukewarm. Add rice. Cook 30 minutes or until rice is tender. Stir occasionally. In a bowl, combine sugar, cornstarch, and eggs. Add vanilla. Beat well. Remove rice mixture from stove. Pour a small amount of milk into the sugar mixture; stir. Pour sugar mixture slowly into rice mixture; mix well. Cook over low heat, stirring constantly, until mixture becomes creamy and thick. Pour into custard dishes. Sprinkle with cinnamon. Cool before serving.
Yield: 6 servings.

NORTHLAND CINNAMON JUMBLES

½ cup soft butter
1 cup granulated sugar
1 egg
¾ cup buttermilk

1 teaspoon vanilla extract
2 cups all-purpose flour, sifted
½ teaspoon baking soda
½ teaspoon salt

Topping:
¼ cup sugar
1 teaspoon ground cinnamon

Preheat oven to 400°. In a mixing bowl, cream butter and sugar thoroughly. Add egg, buttermilk, and vanilla. Beat well. Sift together flour, soda, and salt. Blend into mixture. Chill. Drop batter by rounded teaspoonfuls 2 inches apart on

greased baking sheets. Combine sugar and cinnamon. Sprinkle over jumbles.
Bake 8 to 12 minutes.
Yield: 4 dozen.

OLD-FASHIONED CAKE

¾ cup butter, softened
1 cup sugar
4 eggs
1 cup peach jam
1 teaspoon lemon extract
2½ cups unsifted all-purpose flour

1 teaspoon baking soda
1 teaspoon cinnamon
½ teaspoon baking powder
½ teaspoon allspice
1 cup buttermilk
1 cup currants, dredged in flour

Preheat oven to 350°. Grease three 8-inch round cake pans. In large mixing bowl
cream butter and sugar until light and fluffy. Add eggs, one at a time, beating
well after each addition. Blend in jam and lemon extract. Mix together flour,
baking soda, cinnamon, baking powder, and allspice. Add dry ingredients
alternately with buttermilk; fold in currants. Turn into pans. Bake 25 to 30
minutes until toothpick inserted in center comes out clean. Cool 5 minutes;
remove from pan. Cool completely. Spread Cream Cheese Butter Icing between
layers and on top of cake.
Yield: Three 8-inch layers.

Cream Cheese Butter Icing:
⅓ cup butter, softened
1 3-oz. package cream cheese,
  softened
1 teaspoon grated lemon rind

4½ cups confectioners' sugar
¼ teaspoon salt
3 to 4 tablespoons cream
1 teaspoon vanilla extract

In small mixer bowl cream together butter, cream cheese, and lemon rind until
fluffy. Blend in remaining ingredients until smooth.
Yield: about 2 cups.

ORANGE RICE PUDDING

1 quart milk
1 orange
½ cup uncooked rice
½ cup sugar

½ teaspoon salt
1 cup light cream
2 egg yolks
1 teaspoon vanilla extract

Pour milk into saucepan. Heat to just below the boiling point. Peel orange in one

continuous spiral. Add peel, rice, sugar, and salt to scalded milk. Stir well. Cook, covered, 45 minutes or until rice is tender. Stirring occasionally. Remove orange peel. Combine cream with egg yolks. Mix well. Stir small amount of hot rice into cream mixture; then into hot rice. Continue cooking until mixture thickens, approximately 20 minutes to ½ hour. Stir occasionally. Add vanilla. Pour into individual custard cups. Chill until ready to serve.
Yield: 8 servings.

PEANUT BUTTER QUICKIES

2 cups fine graham cracker crumbs
1 cup sugar

½ cup milk
¾ cup peanut butter

Preheat oven to 350°. In a large bowl, mix graham cracker crumbs, sugar, milk, and peanut butter. With two teaspoons, drop mixture on greased cookie sheet. Bake about 15 minutes, or until cookies are slightly puffed but still soft.
Yield: 3 dozen cookies.

PECAN CHOCOLATE MOUSSE

2 squares unsweetened chocolate, cut in small pieces
1¾ cups milk, scalded
⅓ cup sugar
4 egg yolks, slightly beaten

1 3-oz. package strawberry gelatin
¼ teaspoon salt
½ teaspoon vanilla extract
½ cup pecan meats, coarsely cut
1 cup heavy cream, whipped

Melt chocolate in milk in top part of double boiler; beat mixture until smooth. Remove from heat. Combine sugar and beaten egg yolks. Slowly add to chocolate mixture, stirring vigorously. Return to double boiler. Cook until thickened, stirring constantly. Add gelatin and salt, stirring until gelatin is dissolved. Chill. When slightly thickened, add vanilla. Fold in nuts and whipped cream. Pour into serving dishes. Chill until firm.
Yield: 8 servings.

PINEAPPLE FREEZE

⅔ cup sugar
2 teaspoons grated lemon rind
1 tablespoon lemon juice

2 cups milk
½ cup crushed pineapple

In a mixing bowl combine sugar, lemon rind, and juice. Slowly pour in milk. Stir to dissolve sugar. Add and stir in crushed pineapple. Turn mixture into two refrigerator trays. Freeze until almost firm. Place in a bowl; beat until light and creamy. Return to trays. Freeze until firm.
Yield: 1 quart.

RICE PUDDING WITH KIRSCH FROSTING

3 cups cooked rice	2 tablespoons butter
3 cups milk	2 egg yolks, beaten
⅓ cup sugar	1 teaspoon vanilla extract

Frosting:

¾ cup sugar	2 egg whites
¼ teaspoon cream of tartar	2 teaspoons kirsch
Dash of salt	½ cup chopped maraschino cherries
¼ cup maraschino cherry juice	

In a saucepan, combine rice, milk, sugar, and butter. Cook over medium heat until thick and creamy. Remove from heat. Blend a little of the mixture into beaten egg yolk; then stir in rice. Mix well. Add vanilla extract. Spoon into serving dish. Chill. Before serving, top with kirsch frosting.
Yield: 6 to 8 servings.

Frosting:
Bring first four ingredients to a boil. Cook until a small amount forms a soft ball in cold water (240°). Beat egg whites till stiff but not dry. Gradually pour hot syrup over egg whites, beating constantly. Add kirsch. Serve over pudding. Garnish pudding with chopped cherries.

SHERRY ALMOND BAVARIAN*

1 envelope unflavored gelatin	½ teaspoon almond extract
1¾ cups skim milk	Dash of salt
¼ cup sherry	2 egg whites
¼ cup sugar	

In a saucepan, soften gelatin in skim milk. Heat until dissolved. Remove from heat; pour into mixing bowl. Stir in sherry, 2 tablespoons sugar, almond extract, and salt. Chill until mixture just begins to thicken. Beat egg whites until foamy.

Gradually add remaining sugar, beating well after each addition. Beat until stiff. Fold into gelatin mixture. Chill until firm.
Yield: 4 servings.

*A low-calorie dessert: approximately 150 calories per serving.

TEXAS JAM CAKE

1½ cups all-purpose flour, sifted
 ½ teaspoon baking soda
 ½ teaspoon salt
 ½ teaspoon nutmeg
 ½ teaspoon cinnamon
 ½ cup shortening
 ⅔ cup sugar

 2 egg yolks
 ½ cup buttermilk
 ½ cup blackberry jam
 1 cup walnuts, chopped
 ½ cup raisins
 2 egg whites
 2 tablespoons sugar

Preheat oven to 350°. In a mixing bowl, sift together flour, soda, salt, and spices. Cream shortening and sugar; add egg yolks and beat well. Alternately add dry ingredients and buttermilk. Blend in jam, nuts, and raisins. Beat egg whites, add sugar and beat until stiff; fold into batter. Grease and flour two 8-inch layer cake pans. Pour in batter. Bake for 35-40 minutes. Serve cut in wedges with your favorite hard sauce.
Yield: 8 to 10 servings.

BEVERAGES

APRICOT FLIP

 1 cup milk
 ½ cup canned apricots, drained
 1 cup crushed ice

Combine ingredients in blender. Cover. Blend on high speed until smooth.
Yield: 2 servings.

BUTTERMILK SMOOTHIE*

2 cups cold buttermilk					1 teaspoon Worcestershire sauce

2 cups tomato-vegetable juice,
  chilled

½ teaspoon salt
Dash of hot pepper sauce

Combine ingredients. Chill thoroughly.
Yield: 4 to 6 servings.

*A low-calorie drink: approximately 75 calories per serving.

CHOCOLATE PEANUT BUTTER MILKSHAKE

1 pint vanilla ice cream
½ cup creamy peanut butter

2 cups milk
½ cup instant chocolate flavored mix

Thoroughly combine ice cream and peanut butter. Slowly add milk; then stir in chocolate.
Yield: 4 servings.

CREAMY CHOCOLATE

⅔ cup cocoa
¾ cup sugar
¼ teaspoon salt

1½ cups light cream
4½ cups milk

In a saucepan mix cocoa, sugar, and salt. Add light cream, stirring until well blended. Bring to a boil over medium heat, stirring constantly. Boil until mixture thickens, about 2 minutes. Add milk and continue heating to serving temperature.
Yield: 6 servings.

EGG NOG

4 eggs, separated
½ cup sugar
¼ teaspoon salt

3 cups milk
1 cup whipping cream
½ teaspoon vanilla extract

Beat egg yolks in top part of double boiler. Slowly add ¼ cup sugar and salt, beating constantly. Gradually pour in milk and cream. Cook over hot water, stirring constantly, until mixture thickens and coats a metal spoon. Cool. Add vanilla extract. Chill thoroughly. In mixing bowl beat egg whites to soft peaks, gradually adding remaining sugar. Beat chilled custard until frothy. Fold beaten egg whites into custard.
Yield: about 8 servings.

LIME MILK SCOOP*

2 scoops lime sherbet
2 cups skim milk
Green food color

Soften sherbet. Gradually add milk and a few drops of food color.
Yield: 2 servings.

*A low-calorie drink: approximately 185 calories per serving.

MILK PUNCH

 1 quart milk
¾ cup rum or brandy
 4 eggs

5 tablespoons sifted confectioners'
 sugar
Dash nutmeg

Combine ingredients except nutmeg. Mix well. Sprinkly with nutmeg.
Yield: 4 servings.

MILK SHAKES

LEMON BANANA:
1 pint vanilla ice cream, softened
1 6-oz. can frozen lemonade
 concentrate

1 cup mashed bananas
3 cups milk
1 pint vanilla ice cream

In a mixing bowl, while beating ice cream, gradually add lemonade concentrate.
Blend in bananas. Gradually add milk. Pour into large glasses. Top each with a
scoop of ice cream.
Yield: about 6 cups.

PEACH ALMOND:
2 cups canned peaches and syrup
1 pint vanilla ice cream, softened

2 cups cold milk
¼ teaspoon almond extract

Mash peaches; then place in blender with ice cream, milk, and almond extract.
Beat 2 minutes or until smooth and frothy.
Yield: 4 servings.

PINEAPPLE LEMON:
1 13-oz. can crushed pineapple
  and syrup
2 pints vanilla ice cream

2 cups cold milk
4 teaspoons lemon juice

Combine ingredients in a blender. Beat 2 minutes or until smooth and frothy.
Yield: 4 servings.

MOCHA HOT CHOCOLATE

1 6-oz. package semi-sweet
  chocolate bits
1 tablespoon instant coffee

1 cup boiling water
5 cups milk

In saucepan, melt chocolate bits. Add instant coffee and boiling water. Cook 2
minutes, stirring constantly. Pour in milk, stirring constantly. Heat thoroughly.
Stir occasionally.
Yield: 6 servings.

PARTY-TIME PUNCH

1 quart cold milk
2 pints orange or lime sherbet

1 quart lime-grapefruit
  carbonated beverage, chilled

In a punch bowl, combine milk and 2 pints sherbet. Beat until smooth. Add
carbonated beverage and stir gently, until just blended. Spoon remaining sherbet
on top.
Yield: 28 half-cup servings.

STRAWBERRY MILK

 2 cups cold milk
½ cup frozen strawberries

Strawberries should be partially thawed and undrained. In small bowl, beat both
ingredients together with rotary beater, until well combined.
Yield: 2 servings.

BREADS

BUTTERMILK BREAD

1½ cups buttermilk
1 egg
3 cups biscuit mix
2 tablespoons sugar

1 cup grated Swiss cheese
1 cup sliced pimiento stuffed
  olives, drained
¾ cup chopped walnuts (optional)

Preheat oven to 350°. Combine buttermilk, egg, biscuit mix, and sugar. Beat one minute to blend thoroughly. Gently stir in Swiss cheese, olives, and walnuts. Spoon into a well-greased 9 x 5 x 3-inch loaf pan. Bake 50 to 55 minutes. Cool five minutes before removing from pan. Continue cooling on wire rack.

BUTTER AND EGG ROLLS

1 cup water
½ cup instant nonfat dry milk
½ cup butter
1 teaspoon salt
½ cup sugar

2 cakes compressed yeast
¼ cup water
4 eggs, beaten
1 teaspoon, grated lemon rind
6-6½ cups sifted all-purpose flour

Preheat oven to 400°. In heavy saucepan mix instant nonfat dry milk into water; mix until smooth; scald. Remove from heat; add butter broken into chunks, salt, and sugar. Cool to lukewarm. Soften yeast in water; then add to beaten egg and lemon peel. Combine with scalded, cooled, mixture. Beat in 2 cups of flour until smooth. Add remaining flour gradually, until dough can be handled. Turn out on floured board or pastry cloth and knead until satin smooth, keeping dough as soft as possible. Place in buttered bowl; cover tightly with foil; set in warm place to rise. When it has doubled in bulk (about 1½ hours) punch down; knead on lightly floured board or cloth. Shape ⅔ of dough into 2-inch balls; shape other ⅓ dough into 1-inch balls. Place large ball in greased 2-inch muffin pan; set 1 small ball firmly on top of a large one. Brush with melted butter. Let rise until doubled in size. Bake 12 minutes. Remove from pans at once; cool on cake rack.
Yield: 2½ dozen.

BUTTERMILK HOT CAKES

1 cup all-purpose flour
1 tablespoon sugar
1 teaspoon salt
1 cup buttermilk

½ teaspoon baking soda
1 egg, beaten
2 tablespoons butter, melted

In mixing bowl, sift together flour, sugar, and salt. Add buttermilk. Gradually stir in baking soda, beaten egg, and melted butter. Drop by spoonfuls onto greased, hot griddle. Turn to brown on both sides.
Yield: 14-16 medium pancakes.

CANADIAN BACON GRIDDLE CAKES

1 cup rice flour
2 teaspoons baking powder
½ teaspoon baking soda
½ teaspoon salt

1½ cups buttermilk
2 eggs, well-beaten
¼ cup melted butter
6 slices Canadian bacon

Sift together dry ingredients. Combine buttermilk, eggs, and butter. Add to flour mixture. Beat until smooth. On greased griddle, fry Canadian bacon lightly on both sides. Pour batter over bacon to form griddle cake around each piece of bacon. Cook until bubbles appear; then turn and brown other side.
Yield: 6 griddle cakes.

CRANBERRY QUICK BREAD

1 cup fresh cranberries
1 cup confectioners' sugar
3 cups buttermilk biscuit mix

⅔ cup milk
Light corn syrup

Preheat oven to 375°. Chop cranberries coarsely; combine with confectioners' sugar in a small bowl; allow to stand 10 minutes, stirring several times. Measure biscuit mix into large bowl. Stir milk into cranberries; then add all at once to biscuit mix; stir until blended, then beat 1 minute. Turn out onto a lightly floured pastry board; knead 10 times; shape into an 8-inch round loaf. Place on a large greased cookie sheet. Cut a cross in top of dough with a sharp knife. Bake 40 minutes; brush generously with corn syrup; bake 5 minutes longer, or until brown and shiny.
Yield: 1 loaf.

DATE BUTTERMILK PANCAKES

2 cups sifted all-purpose flour	1 tablespoon sugar
1 teaspoon salt	2 eggs
1 teaspoon baking soda	2 cups buttermilk
¾ teaspoon baking powder	1 tablespoon butter, melted
1 tablespoon cornmeal	1 8-oz. package dates, diced

Sift flour with salt, baking soda, baking powder, corn meal, and sugar. In mixing bowl, beat eggs. Add buttermilk and butter. Add dry ingredients. Beat until smooth. Add dates. Drop batter by spoonfuls on lightly greased hot griddle. Turn to brown on both sides.
Yield: 20-25 pancakes.

GRIDDLE CAKES

2 cups rice flour	2½ cups milk
1½ tablespoons baking powder	1 egg, beaten
1 teaspoon salt	1 tablespoon melted butter
1 tablespoon sugar	

Mix and sift dry ingredients twice. Gradually pour in milk, beating well. Add beaten egg and butter. Beat until smooth. Drop batter by spoonfuls onto lightly greased, medium hot griddle. Turn to brown on both sides.
Yield: about 12 griddle cakes.

MUFFINS

1 cup milk	2 teaspoons baking powder
1 egg	½ teaspoon salt
4 tablespoons shortening, melted	2 tablespoons sugar
2 cups sifted all-purpose flour	

Preheat oven to 425°. Place milk, egg, and shortening in mixing bowl. Beat until well blended. Sift together flour, baking powder, salt, and sugar; add to first mixture. Beat until just moist. Grease 12 3-inch muffin pans. Pour batter into pans. Bake 20-25 minutes.
Yield: 12 muffins.

NEW ENGLAND TEA BREAD

1½ cups fresh cranberries
1¼ cups sugar
2½ cups sifted all-purpose flour
  2 teaspoons baking powder
  1 teaspoon salt

½ teaspoon baking soda
½ teaspoon ground mace
⅓ cup shortening
  1 egg, beaten
½ cup milk

Preheat oven to 350°. Chop cranberries coarsely and combine with ¾ cup of sugar in a small bowl. In large bowl, sift flour, remaining ½ cup sugar, baking powder, salt, baking soda and mace; cut in shortening with a pastry blender until mixture is crumbly. Stir in egg and milk into cranberry mixture; then add all at once to flour mixture, stirring lightly until evenly moist. Spoon into 9 x 5 x 3-inch greased loaf pan. Bake 1 hour, or until a wooden toothpick inserted into center of loaf comes out clean. Allow to ripen 24 hours before slicing.
Yield: 1 loaf.

ONION BUTTER CASSEROLE BREAD

3⅓ cups buttermilk biscuit mix
  ¾ teaspoon dill weed
  ½ teaspoon celery seed
  ⅓ cup butter, softened

½ cup chopped onion
1 egg, beaten
1 cup milk

Topping:
2 tablespoons butter, melted
2 tablespoons grated Parmesan cheese

Preheat oven to 400°. Grease 1½-quart casserole. In medium bowl combine biscuit mix, dill weed, and celery seed. Cut in butter until mixture resembles a fine meal. Stir in onion. Combine egg and milk; add to biscuit mix; stir just until ingredients are moistened. Turn into casserole. About 1-inch from edge of casserole, cut through batter with a knife making a circle. Bake for 30 to 35 minutes, until toothpick inserted in center comes out clean. Brush immediately with Topping. Cool 10 minutes; remove from casserole. Serve warm.
Yield: 1 loaf.

Topping:
Combine all ingredients.

SPICY MANDARIN MUFFINS

1 11-oz. can mandarin oranges,
  cut in half
1½ cups unsifted all-purpose flour
  ½ cup sugar
1¾ teaspoon baking powder
  ½ teaspoon nutmeg
  ½ teaspoon salt
  ¼ teaspoon allspice
  ⅓ cup butter, softened
  ½ cup milk
  1 egg, beaten

Topping:
¼ cup sugar
½ teaspoon cinnamon
⅓ cup butter, melted

Preheat oven to 350°. Line medium muffin cups (2¾-inches in diameter) with paper baking cups. Drain mandarin oranges thoroughly; set aside. In large mixing bowl combine dry ingredients. Cut in butter until mixture resembles a coarse meal. Add milk and egg; stir just until dry ingredients are moistened. Gently stir in oranges. Fill muffin cups ¾ full. Bake 20-25 minutes.
Yield: 12 muffins.

Topping:
Combine sugar and cinnamon. With hot muffins, dip tops into melted butter, then roll in sugar mixture.

INDEX

*low-calorie recipe

*low-calorie recipe

*low-calorie recipe

*low-calorie recipe

*low-calorie recipe

BOOKS OF RELATED INTEREST

Joe Carcione, popular Greengrocer of newspapers, radio and TV, offers his fabulous collection of fresh fruit and vegetable recipes, seasonally arranged, in THE GREENGROCER COOKBOOK. Good food, good nutrition, and good sense from Joe Carcione, your Greengrocer! 252 pages, soft cover, $4.95

Soups from the freezer—soups from the pantry—soups from the barnyard—soups from the sea; Mary and Mike Spencer have written the cookbook to de-Campbellize America—THE ULTIMATE SOUP BOOK. 128 pages, soft cover, $4.95

Gayle and Robert Fletcher Allan's THE EGG BOOK is an extraordinary collection of recipes using eggs as a sole, primary or heavy contributor ingredient. 192 pages, soft cover, $4.95

THE FRENCH GOURMET VEGETARIAN COOKBOOK by Rosine Claire is the cookbook you've been waiting for—a complete collection of truly gourmet vegetarian recipes, French in flavor. 112 pages, soft cover, $3.95

In GONE WITH THE HEARTH, Dorothy Gray traces the rich heritage of antiques, cookbooks and folklore of American kitchenry from Colonial times to the Victorians. 224 pages, soft cover, illustrated with over 100 vintage drawings, $4.95

CELESTIAL ARTS
231 Adrian Road
Millbrae, California